Thomas J. Knight

Disenchanted Night

The Industrialization of Light in the Nineteenth Century

Wolfgang Schivelbusch

Disenchanted Night
The Industrialization of Light in the Nineteenth Century

Translated from the German by
ANGELA DAVIES

The University of California Press
Berkeley / Los Angeles / London

First published in 1988 by
The University of California Press

© Wolfgang Schivelbusch and The University of California Press 1988

First published as *Lichtblicke. Zur Geschichte der künstlichen
Helligkeit im 19. Jahrhundert*, Carl Hanser Verlag
München Wien, 1983

Library of Congress Cataloging-in-Publication Data

Schivelbusch, Wolfgang, 1941–
  Disenchanted night.

  Translation of: Lichtblicke.
  1. Lighting—Social aspects.   2. Cities and towns—Lighting—History—19th
century.   3. Industrialization—History—19th century.   4.
Lamps—History—19th century.
I. Title.
GT440.S3513   1988   392'.36   86–11226
ISBN 0–520–05903–4

Printed in Great Britain by A. Wheaton & Co. Ltd, Exeter

Contents

Illustrations

To Elisabeth Domansky
and with special thanks to
Capers Rubin
who helped so much in the de-Teutonisation of this book

The Lamp

For the 1889 Paris Exposition, Jules Bourdais, a prominent French architect, proposed to erect a tower 360 metres (1,200 feet) high in the centre of Paris, near the Pont-Neuf, with arc-lights strong enough to illuminate the whole city. By this means the *street* lighting of Paris, which at that time consisted of thousands of gas-lamps, was to be transformed into *city* lighting.

This proposal by the builder of the Trocadéro was the subject of detailed discussion, along with another vision involving a tower, that of the bridge construction engineer Gustave Eiffel. Eventually, however, the committee preparing the Exposition decided to accept Eiffel's project. No one doubted that it was technically possible to illuminate the whole of Paris from one source of light. In the end, Eiffel's tower was built, not because it was considered less far-fetched than Bourdais' — on the contrary, contemporaries feared being blinded by such a centralised light source.

Bourdais' Sun Tower (Tour Soleil) is a monument to nineteenth-century fantasies involving light. It is no less impressive for the fact that it was never built and soon fell into oblivion. The proposed tower marks the climax of a development in which earlier technical advances led people to believe that light could be produced in unlimited quantities. They thought in all seriousness of 'turning night into day', to cite a popular expression of the period. But although light was produced in unprecedented quantities and intensities in the nineteenth century, the ideal was never attained. Even Bourdais' tower would only have turned the night into a very dim artificial day.

It makes sense, historically, that this sort of project was conceived, discussed and almost realised in Paris. City of light, *ville lumière* — Paris gained this popular epithet thanks first to the eighteenth-century Enlightenment, of which it was the centre, and then to its brightly lit amusement boulevards, a product of the nineteenth century. On closer inspection, this city of light proves to have been an active centre in the history of artificial lighting. Time and again, it sent out important scientific, technical and psychological impulses. Is there some connection between the philosophical Enlightenment and actual illumination, perhaps along the lines that the philosophical need for enlightenment awakened an interest in real light? If this were the case, we should look for the link between Enlightenment and illumination in the natural sciences of the times, in particular, in chemistry, which was also a Parisian speciality. (Parallels in time and space suggest that Lavoisier's research, which allowed him to arrive at the modern theory of combustion, could be called a chemical 'enlightenment'.) Lavoisier's discovery that flames were not fed by a substance called phlogiston, as had previously been thought, but by the oxygen in the air, opens the more recent history of artificial lighting. Once the true chemical nature of the flame had been recognised, it could be manipulated in a completely new way and no longer had to be accepted as it had existed since time immemorial. With the help of an appropriate chemical apparatus, a flame could now be changed and made to perform at a higher level of efficiency — a process similar to the one that took place at about the same time when James Watt improved the steam engine.

A contemporary of Lavoisier's in Paris rationalised the flame in this way. But first, let us have a look at the development of the flame used exclusively for lighting.

Fire and Flame

Fire is the origin of artificial light. Electric light, too, 'burns' as soon as it is switched on. Fire provided three great cultural services for early mankind: cooking (later expanded to include metallurgy and pottery), heating and lighting. Originally the one undivided fire, around which people gathered after darkness had fallen, fulfilled all three functions. The unity of the primeval fire is the source of the magic that fire possesses for archaic cultures and in mythology.

As civilisation progressed, the original unity dissolved and the functions of fire were separated, although cooking and heating remained connected for a long time. The first element to be separated out was lighting. The most brightly burning logs

The wick
(Detail from George de la Tour, *Sainte Madeleine*,
Musée du Louvre)

would be pulled out of the camp or cooking fire and set up as
fire brands. This experience taught people to distinguish different types of wood in terms of their power of illumination, that
is, by their resin content.

Up to this point, illumination depended entirely on the naturally occurring properties of wood. The next step was a technical innovation. Torches consist of logs of wood that have been
treated artificially with a substance that burns particularly
brightly — resin or pitch. This forms a lump at one end of the
torch. The original log thus lost its significance. From now on it
no longer provided the fuel but simply the shaft or mounting
device.

The candle and the oil-lamp represent the next step in the
technical development of lighting. They are usually described as
a scaling-down and refinement of the torch. 'It was probably
because the aforementioned light sources [i.e. the torch] were

not versatile enough, that the candle was finally invented. Man was searching for a small compact torch which could be carried easily, had a long burning life, required no auxiliary fuel, gave off little smoke or soot, and was easily lighted.'[1] This list of the new qualities of the candle is correct as far as it goes, but it does not mention the fundamentally new technical principle behind the candle.

In the torch, the site of combustion and the fuel are one and the same thing, while in the candle they are clearly separated. From now on the *wick* acts as the sole site of combustion, and it is fed the material the flame needs by the fuel reservoir (the wax cylinder of the candle, the container of oil in the lamp), kept neatly distinct from the flame. The torch had remained a clearly recognisable, if much changed, log of wood from the hearth fire. The flame flickering around a wick for the first time burned totally and exclusively for the purpose of giving light. The wick was as revolutionary in the development of artificial lighting as the wheel in the history of transport.

Psychologically, this technical innovation was extremely significant. Seeing a flame burning around an almost imperceptible wick is a very different experience from seeing a flame flickering around a log or a torch. The log and the torch are physically consumed by the process of burning, but the flame burns around the wick without any visible sign of destruction. The wick remains unchanged (merely requiring to be 'trimmed' from time to time, and even that was unnecessary by the beginning of the nineteenth century), and it is only the fuel feeding it that diminishes. But this takes place at a rate so slow that an observer can perceive it only over a relatively long period of time. In the torch, people experienced the elemental, destructive power of fire — a reflection of their own still-untamed drives. In the candle flame, burning steadily and quietly, fire had become as pacified and regulated as the culture that it illuminated.

The flame cultivated for light thousands of years ago remained essentially unchanged until the eighteenth century. When more light was needed, it was produced simply by multiplying the number of individual lights. Like fireworks, festive illuminations were a standard part of seventeenth- and

1. N.S. Knaggs, *Adventures in Man's First Plastic* (New York, 1947), p. 107.

Ceremonial light display
Philip V of Spain's funeral in Notre Dame Paris, 1746.
(Science Museum, London)

eighteenth-century courtly culture. They were produced by burning thousands of individual lights, consuming sums similar to those spent on other forms of ostentatious waste under the *ancien régime*. In 1688, 24,000 lights were used to illuminate the park of Versailles alone,[2] presumably all wax candles — an extremely costly form of lighting normally used for royal displays. (Feudal light festivals in other forms were also expensive, especially fireworks, which had developed out of the primal bonfire. The motifs of waste and destruction are clearly but inseparably intertwined in an event that combined illumination, bonfire, funeral pyre and fireworks: 'In 1515, when news of Francis I's victory over the Swiss at Marignano reached Rome, one of the Orsinis acquired a whole block of houses, which he crammed with combustible materials and gunpowder and set alight as a bonfire of almost Neroesque proportions.'[3])

The expense of lighting materials limited the use of light in bourgeois households of the time. Artificial light was used for work, not for celebrations; it was employed in a rational, eco-

2. Arthur Lotz, *Das Feuerwerk* (Leipzig, n.d. [1940]), p. 66.
3. Ibid., p. 18.

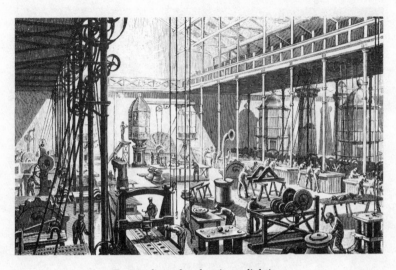

Factory lit up by electric arc lighting
(*Source*: H. Fontaine, *Eclairage à l'électricité*, Paris, 1877)

nomical way, not as a vehicle for conspicuous consumption. It emancipated the working day from its dependence on natural daylight, a process that had begun with the introduction of mechanical clocks in the sixteenth century.[4] For craftsmen, the working day started and finished at set times: in winter, it started so many hours before sunrise and finished a certain number of hours after sunset.

As long as the work that needed to be lit up was tied to individual craftsmen and only the winter morning and evening hours required extra light, the glow provided by traditional candles and oil lamps was adequate. This changed with the introduction of industrial methods of production. Work processes were no longer regulated by the individual worker; they became integrated, comprehensive operations. The new factories needed new sources of light. Artificial light was needed to illuminate larger spaces for longer periods of time. In the facto-

---

4. Wolfgang Nahrstedt, *Die Entstehung der Freizeit, dargestellt am Beispiel Hamburgs* (Göttingen, 1972), p. 117.

ries, night was turned to day more consistently than anywhere else.

Industrial requirements could not be satisfied simply by multiplying traditional sources of light. To light up a cotton mill with hundreds or even thousands of candles in the eighteenth century would have cost as much as the festive illumination of a medium-sized chateau.

As the cost of multiplying the number of individual lights was prohibitive, the only way to increase the amount of light was to heighten the intensity of the individual light source.

Argand: The Modernisation of the Wick

At the end of the eighteenth century the technology of lighting, which had hardly changed for thousands of years, was in a state of flux. The incentive for change was the increased need for light; the immediate trigger was the theory of combustion developed by Lavoisier in the 1770s. He discovered that the oxygen in the air was as necessary for combustion as the carbon in the actual fuel. A new paradigm in chemistry was born, and it stimulated a similar paradigm shift in the technology of lighting. If the air contained a combustible substance of such importance, this factor had to be taken into account in the construction of lamps. In other words, the flame had to receive a bigger air supply than it had previously.

Even before Lavoisier, interest had focused on the actual site of combustion in the lamp. The wick, as we have seen, representing the first revolution in the history of artificial lighting, was still unchanged: a solid round cord of twisted or woven cotton or linen. By the eighteenth century a great deal of experience had been gathered about wicks and ways to improve them. The material, the type of weave and the diameter were all precisely laid down, and people were already going so far as to douse the wick in certain chemicals to make it tougher and more efficient.[5] In 1773 in France, a flat band was used as a wick for

5. Michael Schrøder, *The Argand Burner: Its Origin and Development in France and England 1780–1800* (Odense, 1969), pp. 124–5.

Argand lamp, late eighteenth century
(H.R. d'Allemagne, *Histoire du luminaire*, Paris,
1891)

the first time. This considerably enlarged the flame, giving the effect of a miniature wall of fire — a *surface* of light.[6]

None of these improvements, however, broke out of the traditional paradigm governing combustion and illumination.

In 1783 the chemist and designer Francois Ami Argand publicly unveiled a lamp in Paris that, by contrast, made direct,

6. Ibid., p. 123.

practical use of Lavoisier's findings. 'His lamp was not an isolated technical construction, but represented a philosophical conception of combustion.'[7]

(As with so many eighteenth-century figures, the boundaries between the scientist, the inventor and the entrepreneur were fluid in Argands' case. A 'project maker' combined all these interests and activities. Born in 1750 in Geneva, he studied with the Genevan chemist H. B. de Saussure. When he went to Paris, de Saussure recommended him to Fourcroy and Lavoisier. For some time Argand ran distilleries in Languedoc, with apparent success. He was a close friend and colleague of the Montgolfier brothers, whose hot-air balloon ascents combined sober scientific experiment with elements of a circus act. When Argand's lamp was not an immediate commercial success in Paris, he went straight to England. There he began negotiations with Watt & Boulton, the biggest industrial firm of the time which, he believed, could offer him better business opportunities than he could find in Paris.)

In the same year as the Montgolfier brothers first went up in a balloon, Argand introduced a lamp whose primary innovation was a fundamentally new type of wick. No longer solid, but hollow, the wick in the Argand burner consisted of a flat band rolled up into a small tube. This gave the flame, correspondingly shaped, a double air supply, from outside as well as from inside. Consequently, it burned at a higher temperature, completely consuming the carbon particles left largely unburned by the traditional wick. They had previously gone into the air as soot, dimming the light cast by the flame. Pierre Joseph Macquer, chemist and Fellow of the Académie des Sciences, writing in 1783, gives us an idea of the way in which this new, cylinder-shaped flame affected contemporary perceptions of the light:

> The effect of this lamp is exceptionally beautiful. Its extraordinary bright, lively and almost dazzling light surpasses that of all ordinary lamps, without producing any sort of smoke. I held a sheet of white paper over the flame for quite a long time. A sooty flame would have

---

7. Ibid., p. 96. Schrøder even suggests that the Argand burner might have developed directly from the burners used in chemical laboratories in the eighteenth century (ibid., p. 137).

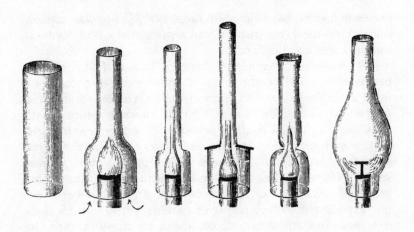

Glass cylinders for Argand lamps
(*Source*: *Buch der Erfindungen, Gewerbe und Industrien*, Leipzig, 1896)

blackened it quickly, but this sheet of paper stayed completely white. In addition, I could not smell the slightest odour near the flame.[8]

The effect of the double air supply was intensified by Argand's second significant innovation: enclosing the flame in a glass cylinder.[9] This acted as a chimney, and also protected the flame from air currents. Enclosed in glass, the flame had at last found its own space, separated from the outside world. Accord-

8. 'L'effet de cette lampe est des plus beaux; sa lumière très blanche, très vive, et presque éblouissante, surpasse de beaucoup celle de toutes les lampes qu'on a imaginées jusque' à présent, du moins à ma connaissance, elle n'est accompagnée d'aucune fumée. J'ai tenu au-dessus de la flamme de cette lampe un papier blanc pendant un temps asser [sic] long pour qu'il fut noirci et enfamé si la flamme eut été fuligineuse; mais ce papier est resté parfaitement blanc; je n'ai non plus remarqué aucune espèce d'odeur au dessus et aux environs de la flamme de la lampe de M. Argand.' Original French quoted from Schrøder, *The Argand Burner*, p. 62. The English version given in the text is translated from the German version in Wolfgang Schivelbusch, *Lichtblicke. Zur Geschichte der künstlichen Helligkeit im 19. Jahrhundert* (Munich and Vienna, 1983), p. 19.

9. In this context, the plagiarism dispute between Argand and his earlier colleagues Quinquet and Lange is not of direct interest. Encouraged by Argand's departure for England in 1783, these two gentlemen gave themselves out as the inventors of the lamp — a case of early 'industrial espionage', as Schrøder says. According to Schrøder, Argand was undoubtedly the original inventor of the lamp, but the addition of the glass cylinder does not seem to be so easily attributable to one or the other of this trio. Schrøder sums up the case on pp. 87–8 of *The Argand Burner*.

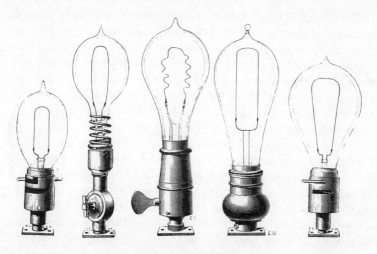

Electric light bulbs
(*Source*: *La Lumière électrique*, 1885)

ing to contemporary accounts, it burned there with amazing calmness and steadiness. The cylinder, wrote one observer, 'allows the flame to burn in complete peace and gives it a remarkable brightness'.[10] In Argand's words, 'the flame did not flicker in the slightest'.[11]

A third device in Argand's burner completed the modernisation of the flame: a mechanism for raising and lowering the wick, thereby varying its length. This made it possible to regulate the supply of oil and thus the intensity of light. Turning the wick up produced a larger flame and more light; turning the wick down had the opposite effect. As Meusnier, a Fellow of the Academy, pointed out in a report, this mechanism made it possible to create a balance 'between the quantity of fuel used and the amount of air necessary for combustion'.[12]

10. '. . . conserve à la flamme une tranquillité inaltérable et lui donne un éclat étonnant', Lange, Argand's colleague and later rival. The original French text is quoted from Schrøder, ibid., p. 110. The English version given in the text is translated from the German version given in Wolfgang Schivelbusch, *Lichtblicke*, p. 20.

11. '. . . impossibilité d'aucune vaccillation dans la flamme'; original French quoted from Schrøder, *The Argand Burner*, p. 207. The English version given in the text is translated from the German version in Schivelbusch, *Lichtblicke*, p. 20.

12. '. . . entre la quantité du combustible consommé et celle de l'air vital qui lui est

The Argand burner was to the nineteenth-century household
what the electric light bulb is to that of the twentieth century. Its
design clearly foreshadowed modern forms of lighting. The
Argand burner possessed primitive equivalents of the elements
technically perfected in an electric bulb: the glass cylinder corresponded to the glass outer casing of an electric bulb, the wick
mechanism to the light switch, and the flame, intensified by the
increased oxygen supply, to the filament.

But this is only one side of the story. Ultimately, the Argand
burner did not transcend traditional lighting technology. In
essence, it remained an *oil-lamp*, that is an open flame burning
around a wick fed by its own fuel reservoir. It was simply an
oil-lamp that had been improved in line with the findings of
modern chemistry. In this form it survived the nineteenth century and, indeed, was to gain a new lease of life after the
discovery of paraffin. The next step in the development of
lighting, involving the application of industrial processes,
opened the modern era in the history of illumination.

Gaslight

Clear, bright, and colourless
(*Monthly Magazine*, 1807)

La flamme est sortie blanche et brillante, l'oeil
avait peine à en soutenir l'éclat.
(*Almanach sous verre*, 1812)

It completely penetrates the whole atmosphere
. . . appears as natural and pure as daylight.
(Newspaper report, 1815)

Das Gaslicht ist zu rein für das menschliche
Auge, und unsere Enkel werden blind
werden.
(Ludwig Börne, *c.* 1824)

---

fourni'; original French quoted from Schrøder, *The Argand Burner*, p. 118. The English
version in the text is translated from the German version in Schivelbusch, *Lichtblicke*, p. 20.

Le gaz a remplacé le soleil.

(Jules Janin, 1839)

In the dazzling brightness of gaslight, the first thing people wanted to know was what had happened to the wick. 'Do you mean to tell us that it will be possible to have a light without a wick?', an MP asked the gas engineer William Murdoch at a hearing in the House of Commons in 1810.[13] What to ordinary perceptions seemed contrary to the nature of combustion was explained prominently in the numerous manuals on gas lighting that were published soon after. For example, we read in Samuel Clegg's *Practical Treatise on the Manufacture and Distribution of Coal-Gas*, a standard work that went through five editions, that

> the whole difference between the greater process of the gas-light operation and the miniature operation of a candle or a lamp, consists in having the distillatory apparatus at the gaslight manufactory, at a distance, instead of being in the wick of the candle or lamp — in having the crude inflammable matter decomposed, previous to the elastic fluid being wanted, and stored up for use, instead of being prepared and consumed as fast as it proceeds from the decomposed oil, wax, or tallow; and lastly, in transmitting the gas to any required distance, and igniting it at the burner or lamp of the conducting tube, instead of burning it at the apex of the wick.[14]

In his *Handbuch für Steinkohlengas-Beleuchtung* (Manual of Coal-Gas Lighting), Schilling expresses the same idea more briefly and more poetically: 'The flame of a candle or a lamp is . . . a true microcosm of a gas-works. It operates so reliably and silently in the tiny space at the end of a wick that for many centuries its presence went unnoticed.'[15]

It had been known since the seventeenth century at least that distilling coal or wood produces an inflammable gas. The first description of this phenomenon appears in a letter written by John Clayton, an amateur chemist, to Robert Boyle before 1691, though it was not published until 1739 in the journal *Philosophical Transactions of the Royal Society*. Clayton writes:

13. Samuel Smiles, *Lives of the Engineers: Boulton and Watt* (London, 1874), p. 349.

14. Samuel Clegg, Jr, *A Practical Treatise on the Manufacture and Distribution of Coal-Gas*, 1st edn (London, 1841), pp. 53–4.

15. N.H. Schilling, *Handbuch für Steinkohlengas-Beleuchtung*, 2nd edn (Munich, 1866).

I got some coal, and distilled it in a retort in an open fire. At first there came over only phlegm, afterwards a black oil, and then likewise a spirit arose, which I could no ways condense; but it forced my lute, or broke my glasses. Once, when it had forced my lute, coming close thereto in order to try to repair it, I observed that the spirit which issued out, caught fire at the flame of the candle, and continued burning with violence as it issued out in a stream, which I blew out and lighted again alternately for several times. I then had a mind to try if I could save any of this spirit; in order to which I took a turbinated receiver, and, putting a candle to the pipe of the receiver, whilst the spirit arose, I observed that it catched [sic] flame, and continued burning at the end of the pipe, though you could not discern what fed the flame. I then blew it out and lighted it again several times.[16]

'Inflammable air' or 'spirit', as this gas was called, was officially known by 1739 at the latest. But even though people knew what it was and how to make it, no one put this knowledge to practical use in the decades that followed. Like many mechanical inventions of the period, gas was used only for fun. 'When I had a mind to divert strangers or friends', Clayton's letter continues,

I have frequently taken one of these bladders [i.e. gas containers made of animals' bladders] and pricked a hole therein with a pin, and compressing gently the bladder near the flame of a candle till it took fire, it would then continue flaming till all the spirit was compressed out of the bladder; which was the more suprising because no one could discern any difference in the appearance between these bladders and those which are filled with common air.

The playful phase in the history of gaslight came to an end around 1800, with the sudden discovery that it was suitable for lighting the new English factories. At the time, these were sprouting like mushrooms, and they soon generated a great demand for light.

Modern gas lighting began as industrial lighting. It shares this industrial origin with the other great technological innovation of the nineteenth century, the railway. Railways were used to

---

16. *Philosophical Transactions of the Royal Society for the Year 1739*, vol.XLI, quoted from T.S. Peckston, *The Theory and Practice of Gas-Lighting* (London, 1819), p. 92.

transport coal in Newcastle before they become a general means of transportation. Both were natural outgrowths of the English industrial landscape, and this was shaped by coal. The coal industry gave birth to the Industrial Revolution in England.

This view is held by many historians, most strongly by John Nef,[17] and there is much to support it. Around 1600 England's industrial and technological position in Europe was marginal, even parasitical; a century later the positions were reversed. The driving force behind this change was England's enormous coal deposits. The exhaustion of wood supplies at the time made coal increasingly important, and England's reserves gave her an edge over the rest of Western Europe. The introduction of coal and coal-based technology into areas of production that had previously been wood-based resulted in a great technological spurt. John R. Harris writes:

> As it became clear in many segments of the economy that coal contained the potential of more efficient production and lower costs, industries that had not yet adopted coal looked to those that had made the change most successfully and borrowed and adapted techniques and apparatus already available. Moreover, each industry that switched to coal found it necessary to innovate and to modify existing equipment and procedures in order to accommodate the new fuel. Higher temperatures attained by burning coal, for example, demanded modification in the design of furnaces and made the need for improved refractory materials urgent.[18]

If the industrial culture of Europe before the eighteenth century was materially and technologically *wood-based*, as Werner Som-

17. John U. Nef., *Rise of the British Coal Industry*, 2 vols. (London, 1932).

18. John R. Harris, 'The Rise of Coal Technology', *Scientific American*, August 1974, p. 96. We should also like to refer to Maurice Daumas' approach. He suggests pursuing the 'inner logic' of any given technology and names the whole complex surrounding coal as a model: 'The close connections between mining, the steam engine and the production of iron using coke are one of the classic examples. A study of horizontal and vertical interlinkages furnishes further evidence. For example, an obvious logical link exists between the distillation of coke and the production of illuminating gas and between this and the preparation of artificial dyes and the development of the internal combustion engine. One also finds a link when investigating the influence of the steam engine on the forms of the first gas engines and of Froment's electro-magnetic motors' (M. Daumas, 'L'histoire des techniques: son objet, ses limites, ses méthodes', *Documents pour l'histoire des techniques*, 7, 1969; translated here from the German version in R. Rürup and K. Hausen (eds.), *Moderne Technikgeschichte*, Cologne, 1975, p. 41).

bart has suggested, then developments in England since the seventeenth century must be described as *coal-based*.

Let us go back to gas lighting. Gas could be produced without any technical innovations. It was obtained by more or less the same process as the one that turned coal into coke, first used by Abraham Darby early in the eighteenth century. After all, coke is nothing but coal that has been distilled. For a long time, only one of the by-products of this process was used for something else — tar for caulking ships — while the gas given off simply blew away in the air. The production of gas for lighting merely involved exploiting a previously ignored waste product. This economically attractive quality, combined with its power of illumination, made gas a suitable fuel for industrial lighting.

The first gas lighting systems were installed in the very stronghold of British industry, Watt & Boulton of Soho near Birmingham. The owners of this firm had already shown their interest in lighting innovations when they started producing Argand burners in the 1780s. They knew the inventor of the Argand burner personally; he had come to England because he hoped it would offer him better commercial opportunities than France had done. At Watt & Boulton, it was the William Murdoch mentioned above who took the lead in gas lighting, more or less on his own initiative. (Around 1800 Murdoch built the first functional model of a steam locomotive — another example of the nineteenth-century affinity between railways and gas lighting. Carl Gustav Carus calls gas and steam the 'two main driving forces of history'.) Murdoch's experiments in the last years of the eighteenth century illustrate how gas lighting progressed from an experimental to an industrial stage. We can see clearly how the inherent qualities of gas technology influenced later developments. There was no fully developed system from the start that kept the production, storage, distribution and consumption of gas clearly separate from each other.

Murdoch began by heating coal in the small glass retorts that were commonly used in the science laboratories of the day. Clayton had probably used them too. After some time Murdoch switched to larger iron containers. Even these, however, did not hold more than 15 pounds of coal.[19] Like Clayton and other

19. William Matthews, *An Historical Sketch of the Origin, Progress and Present State of Gas-Lighting* (London, 1827), p. 24.

early-eighteenth-century experimenters, Murdoch filled the gas
produced in this way into balloon-like containers. The chemist
William Henry describes how they were carried around like a
lamp or a candle. 'Bags of leather, and of varnished silk, bladders, and vessels of tinned iron, were filled with the gas, which
was set fire to and carried about from room to room, with a view
of ascertaining how far it could be made to answer the purposes
of a moveable or transferable light.'[20]

But this form of storage and distribution soon proved to be
unsuitable for gas. (Transportable gas was not feasible until
compression techniques became available, and even then it was
only developed for very limited purposes.) Murdoch saw that
he would have to connect the site of production to the site
where gas was consumed. He did this with pipes, which took
the gas from the retort, where it was produced, to a gasometer,
where it was stored. From here it could be drawn off for use at
any time. More pipes conveyed the gas to the site of combustion. Valves regulated the whole process. Murdoch installed the
first system of this kind in the forge at Soho in 1802; a second
one, built for a Manchester cotton mill in 1805, was technically
more complicated. Here gas technology, in its basic outlines,
was already fully developed. The system designed for Phillips &
Lee in Manchester consisted of retorts, a gasometer, pipelines,
valves and, as a further improvement, a mechanism for purifying the gas. The journal *Philosophical Transactions of the Royal
Society*, which seventy years earlier had published the report of
Clayton's first experiment, printed Murdoch's description of his
perfected system in 1808:

> The gas as it rises from them [the retorts] is conveyed by iron pipes
> into large reservoirs, or gazometers, where it is washed and purified,
> previous to its being conveyed through other pipes, called mains, to
> the mill. These mains branch off into a variety of ramifications
> (forming a total length of several miles), and diminish in size, as the
> quantity of gas required to be passed through them becomes less.[21]

This system is the prototype of all later gas-works, the only
differences being in scale and technical detail. At this stage, we

20. Quoted from Peckston, *Theory and Practice of Gas-Lighting*, p. 95.
21. *Philosophical Transactions of the Royal Society* (1808), p. 125.

must remember, gaslight was used exclusively for lighting factories. Neither Murdoch nor his employers, Boulton and Watt,
thought of any possible application outside industry. They
knew the advantages of gaslight, but only as they applied to
factory work. Murdoch pointed out that 'its being free from the
inconvenience and danger, resulting from the sparks and fre-
quent snuffing of candles, is a circumstance of material importance, as tending to diminish the hazard of fire, to which cotton
mills are known to be much exposed'.[22] And the 'peculiar
softness and clearness of this light', made much of by Murdoch,
was also seen solely as an advantage in industry. As Murdoch
said, these qualities brought the new light 'into great favour
with the work people'.

Before gaslight could move out of the factory and be put to
more general use, an invisible barrier had to be overcome. Gaslight had to be seen from a point of view and in the context of
experiences quite different from those of the English industrial
pioneers. This happened in Paris.

The 'Thermolamp'

France had not experienced anything like England's industrialisation. Coal led a marginal existence there and well into the
nineteenth century it remained a *produit revolutionnaire*.[23] Wood
continued to be the most important fuel.

In this situation Philippe Lebon, a graduate of the École des
ponts et chaussées, had been experimenting with gas distilled
from wood since the early 1790s. Lebon (1767–1804) was an
inventor and 'project-maker' like François Argand: scientifically
trained, in touch with the leading chemists of his day (Fourcroy,
Guyton de Morveau) but also interested in the practical application — put more bluntly, the commercial exploitation — of his
results. As he lacked the industrial framework within which
Murdoch operated, his motives and goals were necessarily
different. For Lebon, gas lighting was not an industrial development — as we have said, France did not yet have any industry.

22. Ibid.
23. C. Fohlen, in 'Charbon et Sciences Humaines', *Colloque international de l'Université de Lille en mai 1963* (Lille, 1963), p. 148.

Instead, for Lebon, gas lighting possessed its own intrinsic value, as something that contributed to the civilisation and progress of humanity. Accordingly, he saw gas production less as the exploitation of a previously neglected waste product than as the realisation of a philosophical principle. (Lebon's concept of gas relates to Murdoch's as do Saint Simonianism and utopian socialism to English political economy. In both cases the prose of English economy was translated into the poetry of French humanitarian industrial systems.)

Lebon was interested in gas as something that did not have the disadvantages and impurities of naturally occurring fuels. In 1799 he published a work entitled 'Moyens nouveaux d'employer les combustibles plus utilement et à la chaleur et à la lumière et d'en recueillir les divers produits' (New methods for employing heating and lighting fuels more profitably and for collecting the various constituents), in which he described his starting point:

> Up to now, we have not been able to resolve fuel into various components. We have not possessed the technical means to separate out the constituents that help, or even hinder, the production of heat and light, which could perhaps be useful for other purposes. These substances include, above all, the pyroligneous acid contained in wood, that can be used to advantage in the production of porcelain blue as well as in various other operations. Up to now we have not been able to use the elements necessary for combustion separately and in a form so pure that a completely even heat and light are produced. We have not sufficiently mastered the principle upon which the production of heat and light rests (inflammable gas, also known as hydrogen gas). We have not been able to store it in order to use it for balloons or other purposes; we cannot conduct it at will so that its capacity for producing light and heat can be used at other, distant places.[24]

24. 'Jusqu'à présent nos moyens n'ont point offert séparément à notre disposition les diverses parties constituantes du combustible. Nous n'avons pu recueillir celles de ces parties qui étaient ou inutiles ou nuisibles à la combustion à la chaleur et à la lumière et qui pouvaient être précieuses pour d'autres usages. Parmi celles-ci on doit compter spécialement l'Acide pyroligneux contenu dans le bois et qui s'emploie avec avantage à former les chaux métalliques et diverses autres opérations. Nous n'avons pu offrir isolément à la combustion chacune de ces parties qui en était susceptible, régler une opération qui devênait trop compliquée, en coercer et recueillir les produit et obtenir des effets constants de lumière et de chaleur. Nous n'avons pu gouverner à tel point le principe qui poduit et de

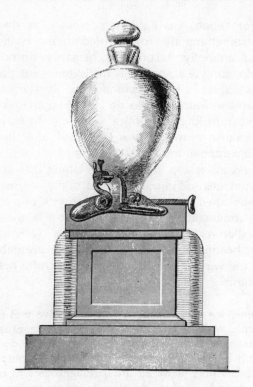

Thermolamp, late eighteenth century
(*Source*: H.R. d'Allemagne, *Historie du luminaire*,
Paris, 1891)

For Lebon distilling natural fuel meant reordering the chaos of nature by rational, scientific principles. The gas made this way was seen as pure energy, just as a hundred years later electricity would be seen as pure (in contrast to gas, which had become 'dirty' in the meantime).

Lebon's 'thermolamp' was technically almost identical with

la lumière et de la chaleur (le gaz inflammable ou hydrogène) que l'on put à son gré le recuillir, soit pour le destiner aux aérostats, soit pour tout autre usage, le distribuer, modifier le nombre et la forme de ses jets, l'enflammer et lui faire porter à toute distance du foyer la lumière et la chaleur.' The original French is quoted from Charles Hunt, *A History of the Introduction of Gas Lighting* (London, 1907), p. 52. The English version in the text is translated from the German version given in Wolfgang Schivelbusch, *Lichtblicke*, p. 28.

Murdoch's system: gas was produced in a retort, stored in a container and conveyed to the site of combustion by pipes. The difference lay in the intended application. The thermolamp emitted not only light but also heat, and beyond this, was to serve as a general energy source. The title under which Lebon published a description of his apparatus in 1801 makes it sound like a technical utopia: 'Thermolampe ou poêle qui chauffe et éclaire avec économie et offre avec plusiers produits précieux une force motrice applicable à toutes sortes de machines' (Discovery of a thermolamp or storage stove that heats every room in the whole house, provides light and can be used to give all machines locomotive power). The text describes a house with a centralised lighting and heating system:

> By an arrangement so very easy, a single stove may supersede all the chimneys of a house. The inflammable gas is ready to extend every where the most sensible heat and the softest lights, either joined or separated at our pleasure. In a moment we can make our lights pass from one chamber into another — an advantage as commodious as oeconomical — and which our common chimneys can never be made to furnish. No sparks, coals or soot will incommode us any longer. Neither can cinders ashes coals or wood, render our apartments black or dirty nor require the least care. Night and Day we may have fire in our rooms without any servant being obliged to enter, to stir it or to watch over its dangerous effects.[25]

For practical purposes, the thermolamp was a flop. Lebon installed one in his Paris house and opened it to the public, charging three francs admission. It aroused the same sort of interest as William Trevithick's steam engine. At roughly the same time in England, Trevithick put on public display a steam locomotive driving around in a circle, and also charged for admission. It is one of the ironies of history that the two

25. The English text is quoted from *Description of the Thermolamp invented by Lebon of Paris, Published with remarks by F. A. W.* [Winsor], in English, German and French (Brunswick, 1802), pp. 11–12. The original French text is quoted in Henry-René d'Allemagne, *Histoire du luminaire* (Paris, 1891), pp. 557–8). The title of this paper given in English in the text is translated from the German: 'Nachricht von einer ganz neuen außerordentlichen, vom pariser National-Institut geprüften, und durch ein Erfindungs-Patent authorisierten *Entdeckung einer Thermo-Lampe* oder eines *Spar-Ofens*, welcher alle Zimmer im ganzen Hause heizt, beleuchtet, und allen Maschinen eine Bewegkraft zu geben, anwendbar ist. Erfunden von Hrn. Phillip Lebon' (Stadtamhof, 1802).

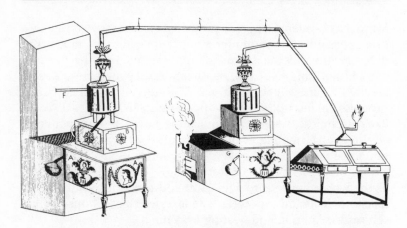

Two thermolamps (1802).
A fire lit in the furnace (A) heats up the retort (B), from which the gas
passes into the condenser (C). From there, a pipe conveys it to the site
of combustion. Excess gas is removed via a pipe (F) which takes it to a
storage container or releases it unused into the air.
(*Source*: T.M. Daisenberger, *Beschreibung der daisenbergerschen
Thermolampe*, Stadt am Hof, 1802)

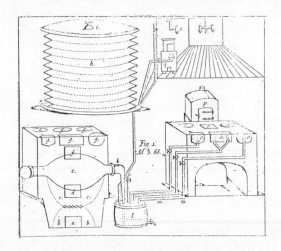

Thermolamp (1803)
Bottom left: the retort, from which the distilled gas is conveyed to a
container in which it is purified (1). Then it passes into a still small
gasometer where it is stored (h). From there it is taken to the stove
(o, p) and to the lights (r, s).
(*Source*: Z. Winzler, *Die Thermolampe in Deutschaland*, Brno, 1803)

arguably most important innovations of the nineteenth century first appeared in public as something like a circus act.

Even if the thermolamp was not an immediate success, it did for the first time point to the possibility of *central* lighting and heating systems. It was a remarkable blend of traditional and progressive ideas. Lebon's concept of a universal energy source to provide light, heat and power was ahead of its time, but he was still governed by tradition in restricting the central supply to one house. The idea of a thermolamp for a whole city, or at least for a particular district, did not occur to him. The thermo-lamp remained a Heath Robinson-like central supply station, inspired by the same spirit of individualism as the equally self-sufficient gas lighting systems in English factories.

Central Supply

By about 1800 the foundations for the gas lighting of the future were fully developed. The technology existed in Watt & Boul-ton's industrial installations; the idea of a more general use, not restricted to factories, was born with Lebon's thermolamp. In retrospect, we can see these developments as two loose ends, waiting to be tied up to create modern gas lighting. This was achieved by Friedrich Albert Winsor, a German 'project-maker' who had migrated to England. (Originally his name was Win-zer, not to be confused, as he so often is by historians of the gas industry, with the Austrian gas pioneer and follower of Lebon, Zacharias Andreas Winzler.) Winsor first familiarised himself with Lebon's work. Still in Germany, he published a translation of Lebon's book on the thermolamp in 1802. A little later in London he initiated a campaign that was to go on for years. Its aim was to promote gas lighting by setting up a company to deliver gas to consumers. Winsor eventually achieved his aim in 1810, when his company received a charter and began trading.

Winsor cannot be pigeonholed as a scientist-inventor, or as a capitalist entrepreneur. Without possessing the qualities of either, he was able to mediate between them, acting as a catalyst. According to contemporary accounts, Winsor had little know-ledge of the matter he was so interested in promoting. 'He possessed scarcely any knowledge of chemistry, and was so deficient in mechanical information, that he was unable to give proper directions for the construction of the apparatus', wrote William Matthews in the first history of gas lighting, published in 1827.[26] The *Edinburgh Review* accused him of 'ignorance, quackery, extravagance, and false calculation'.[27] His enterprise was compared to the scandalous South Sea Bubble of 150 years earlier. But despite this unpleasantness, the public displayed interest in his lectures and demonstrations (which included illuminating the Mall). 'Their brilliance was surprisingly attractive, and allured the public to inspect them', noted William Matthews (after venting his criticism), 'and his explanations and illustrations so far elucidated the subject of gas as to enable others to form some estimate of its utility as an agent for producing light. His representations may justly be deemed extravagant and deceptive, and certainly exposed him to ridicule and suspicion; but it must be allowed that his efforts tended, in a high degree, to fix public attention to Gas-Lighting.'[28]

Ultimately, despite the success of gas — or perhaps because of it — Winsor got as little out of it as Lebon, from whose pioneering work he had profited. After Winsor had founded his company and business proved to be good, 'serious' entrepreneurs took over the directorship, and Winsor was squeezed out. He decided to move on and repeat his English experience somewhere else. Paris, the other great metropolis of the time, seemed an obvious choice. Winsor tried to use again the techniques that had worked in London: staging practical demonstrations, giving lectures and publishing pamphlets. In 1816 he installed gaslight in a public house in the Passage des Panoramas as a demonstration, but it was as unsuccessful as all his later ventures in Paris. Soon after this, his company went bankrupt. Winsor died, impoverished, in Paris in 1830.

Winsor was not the original inventor of gas lighting and, perhaps, not a serious capitalist entrepreneur. But he established the concept that allowed gas lighting to make the transition from individual to general use: the idea of supplying consumers of gas from a central production site by means of gas

26. Matthews, *Historical Sketch*, p. 28.
27. Chandler and Lacey, *The Rise of the Gas Industry in Britain*, p. 130.
28. Matthews, *Historical Sketch*, p. 30.

mains. The idea was, in fact, nothing new. As the title of one of Winsor's many advertising pamphlets shows, the water supply provided the model: 'A National Light and Heat Company, for providing streets and houses with light and heat, on similar principles, as they are now supplied with water.' The author of the first analytical description of gas lighting, Frederick Accum, a colleague of Winsor's and also a German emigré, makes a special point of this analogy: 'By means of gas we may have a pure and agreeable light at command in every room of our house, just as we have the command of water.'[29] The translator of the German edition added an explanatory note for his readers, who were unfamiliar with a centralised water supply: 'In England, many private houses are so arranged, with pipes etc. inside the walls, that in almost every room one can obtain water at any time simply by opening a tap.' London had been supplied with tap water since the early eighteenth century. A report written in 1726 by de Saussure, a Swiss traveller, however, shows that London's water supply initially consisted of a large number of fountains rather than of taps in the modern sense: 'In every street there is a large principal pipe made of oak wood and little leaden pipes are adapted to this principal pipe to carry water into all houses. Every private individual may have one or two fountains in his house, according to his means, and pays so much a year for each fountain.'[30]

The technical principle behind a central gas supply for a whole city is the same as the one behind a thermolamp supplying a single house. The only difference is in the size of the system and the length of the pipes. A thermolamp operated according to the principles of the central heating system known since Roman times, and a centralised gas supply was simply a public version of the same thing. And as the Austrian Andreas Zacharias Winzler, an enthusiastic supporter of the thermolamp, foresaw correctly, the notion of expansion was inherent in the idea of the thermolamp:

---

29. Frederick Accum, *A Practical Treatise on Gas-Light; Exhibiting a Summary Description of the Apparatus and Machinery Best Calculated for Illuminating Streets, Houses, and Manufactories* . . . (London, 1815), p. 111.

30. Quoted from Frederick William Robins, *The Story of Water Supply* (London, New York and Toronto, 1946), p. 106.

The installation of thermolamps in large hospitals, in barracks, courts, offices, factories, monasteries, convents and communal buildings of all sorts . . . obviously follows quite naturally. It is also easy to appreciate that this inestimable invention could be used with great advantage to light the streets. But the fact that one stove could provide light and heat for all the houses of a whole municipality deserves special mention here because there might be cases in which this sort of arrangement would be of the greatest benefit to the inhabitants of whole villages.[31]

Expanding a thermolamp into a gas-works was not a technical innovation, but it did have far-reaching consequences. Once a house was connected to a central gas supply, its autonomy was over. The thermolamp had merely centralised heating and lighting within one house; now these systems were relocated outside the house, at a distance beyond the control of the paterfamilias. With a public gas supply, domestic lighting entered its industrial — and dependent — stage. No longer self-sufficiently producing its own heat and light, each house was inextricably tied to an industrial energy producer.

This loss of domestic autonomy is part of the larger dissolution of the 'total household'.[32] A market and exchange economy, based on the division of labour, absorbed ever more activities and functions originally performed by individual households. Removing the production of light and heat from the house gave this process a new quality. When the household lost its hearth fire, it lost what since time immemorial had been the focus of its life. Although refined and civilised over the centuries in the form of stoves, oil lamps and candles, fire had always remained clearly and physically recognisable as not merely a product but also the soul of the house. As Gaston Bachelard puts it, 'the lamp is the spirit that watches over every room. It is the centre of the house. A house without a lamp is as unthinkable as a lamp without a house'.[33]

Bachelard is referring here only to the domestic oil-lamp. Its replacement by industrially produced gas lighting affected peo-

---

31. Zacharias Andreas Winzler, *Die Thermolampe in Deutschland* (Brno, 1803), p. 155.

32. See Otto Brunner, "Das "ganzes Haus" und die alteuropäische "Ökonomik"", in *Neue Wege zur Sozialgeschichte* (Göttingen, 1956), pp. 33–61. The expression 'ganzes Haus', here translated as 'total household', was coined by the folklorist W.H. Riehl.

33. Gaston Bachelard, *La Flamme d'une chandelle* (Paris, 1961), p. 8.

ple in much the same way as did the replacement of the coach by the railway. Gaslight and the railway were often compared in the nineteenth century. These two industrial innovations came into the world at the same time, with similar technologies. 'A gas-work, like a railway, must be viewed as one entire and indivisible machine; the mains in one case being analogous to the rails in the other.'[34] To contemporaries it seemed that industries were expanding, sending out tentacles, octapus-like, into every house. Being connected to them as consumers made people uneasy. They clearly felt a loss of personal freedom. The railway put an end to the freedom of guiding an individual conveyance at will. Similarly, gaslight made it impossible for people to become absorbed in contemplating the 'individual' flame of an oil-lamp or candle. Railway travellers, no longer living in the landscape through which they were being transported, felt like parcels in a pneumatic tube. People gazing at a gaslight no longer lost themselves in dreams of the primeval fire;[35] if anything, they were thinking of the gas bill. As a rule, though, no one looked at the gas flame any more at all.

In economic organisation, too, the railways and the gas industry led to the loss of individual entrepreneurial freedom. The principle of free competition could not be reconciled with this new technology. Attempts to uphold it at all costs produced absurd, inefficient and ultimately chaotic conditions. At first, competing gas companies laid their mains in the same areas. 'It was not at all unusual for three, four or even five different companies to have mains in the same street.'[36] Later, regions were divided into districts, for which individual companies received monopolies. On the Continent, where political traditions were more centralised and less liberal, the railway and gas systems developed differently from the start. Strict governmental supervision ensured that private companies co-ordinated their operations. In France, the railway network was centrally planned from the beginning — various private companies received monopolies for various lines. The same was true of the gas industry. The first regulations concerning the gas industry

34. J.O.N. Rutter, *Gas-Lighting: Its Progress and Its Prospects* (London, 1849), p. 54.
35. Bacheland, *La Flamme*, p. 3.
36. George Livesay, quoted from Chandler and Lacey, *The Rise of the Gas Industry in Britain*, p. 74.

Retort room in a London gas-works, 1821
(*Source*: C. Mackenzie, *One Thousand Experiments in Chemistry*, London,
1822)

laid down by the Prefect of the Département Seine prescribed
that 'only one company may construct its mains in any one
street'.[37] Later provisions established this system in ever greater
detail. In 1839 Paris was finally divided into districts, in which
individual companies exercised their monopolies.[38] Germany
developed in much the same way.

Expansion

The speed with which the gas industry took hold varied with
the speed of industrialisation in the different European countries. England was the first to come under its thrall, and the
industry developed most quickly there; the Continent lagged
behind.

37. Henri Besnard, *L'Industrie du gaz à Paris depuis ses origines* (Paris, 1942), p. 36.
38. Ibid., p. 42.

The first gas-works, London, 1814
Left: the storage container (gasometer); under the chimney the
transverse retorts; beneath these the coal store, purifying plant
and basin to catch the tar given off as a by-product of the
process.
(*Source*: F. Accum, *A Practical Treatise on Gas-Light*, London, 1815)

Within a few years, London became the first metropolis to be
largely supplied with gas. In 1814 there was one company,
founded by Winsor, which possessed a single gasometer with a
capacity of 14,000 cubic feet. Eight years later, in 1822, there
were already four companies and forty-seven gasometers with a
total volume of almost one million cubic feet.[39] By this time, 200
miles of mains with a diameter of eighteen inches had been
laid.[40] Later, gas-works expanded again. The development of
gasometers, one of the most potent industrial symbols of the
nineteenth century, illustrates this most clearly. In the 1820s
gasometers were rarely bigger than 20,000 cubic feet. By the
1860s their average size was one million cubic feet. After London, the gas industry spread to the rest of England: 'Gas had

39. Matthews, *Historical Sketch*, p. 145.
40. Peckston, *Theory and Practice of Gas-Lighting*, pp. 294–5.

become common in London in 1816, and by 1819 gas works were in operation throughout the country.'[41] In the mid-1820s most of the big cities were supplied with gas; by the late 1840s it had reached the small towns and even villages.[42]

The gas industry spread incomparably more slowly in France and Germany. As Winsor's failure in Paris shows, there was no market there yet for the new type of light. Developments after Winsor's time confirm that this remained true for years. Companies founded in the 1820s were 'loin de prospérer'; between 1820 and 1835, bankruptcies of gas companies accounted for capital losses of 8 million francs.[43] Only from 1829 did gas begin to be used for street lighting, and then its use spread at snail's pace. The first streets and squares with gas lighting were the Place du Carousel, Rue de Rivoli, Rue de la Paix, Place Vendôme and the Palais Royal. Not until the mid-1840s was gas lighting so well established in Paris that, as the historian Henri Besnard declares, it enjoyed the 'confiance du public'.[44] Given Paris's traditions of light, this was a surprising delay. The French historian Allemagne later found it painful 'to have to record that other countries valued the advantages of Lebon's great invention more highly than we did. Our neighbours quickly found a variety of uses for it'.[45]

In Germany progress was just as slow. Although people were experimenting with gaslight there — Lampadius, for example, and Winzler — the industry as such was imported from Britain. The Imperial Continental Gas Association, established in England solely as an export company, set up gas-works in Hanover, Berlin, Aachen, Cologne and Vienna in the 1820s. Soon domestic industry took up the idea, but there were only twenty-four gas-works in operation by 1850.[46] The breakthrough did not occur until the 1850s, marked most clearly, perhaps, by the

41. Chandler and Lacey, *The Rise of the Gas Industry in Britain*, p. 71.
42. W.J. Liberty, 'The Centenary of Gas Lighting', *Illuminating Engineer*, vol. 6, 1913 (London), p. 185. The exact figures are as follows: in 1823, fifty-three English cities had gas companies (Georg Moritz Sigismund Blochman, *Beiträge zur Geschichte der Gasbeleuchtung*, Dresden, n.d. [1871], p. 99); around 1850 more than 700 companies had a share of the market (Rutter, *Gas-Lighting*, p. 26; Blochmann, *Beiträge*; by 1868 there were 1,134 (ibid.).
43. Besnard, *L'Industrie du gaz à Paris*, p. 24.
44. Ibid., p. 32.
45. d'Allemagne, *Histoire du luminaire*, p. 576.
46. Schilling, *Handbuch für Steinkohlengas-Beleuchtung*, p. 13.

Gasometer, about 1870
(Archiv für Kunst und Geschichte, Berlin)

foundation of the *Journal für Gasbeleuchtung* (Journal of gas lighting) in 1858. Nevertheless, the English influence continued for a
long time. For example, as late as 1862 more than 40 per cent of
the coal used in German gas production was imported from
England.[47] At this time London alone consumed twice as much
gas as the whole of Germany.[48]

The Danger of Explosion

During his visit to London, Carl Gustav Carus recorded the
following impression of the industrial landscape on the Thames:
'masses of houses, warehouses, big breweries and enormous
iron gasometers, standing free like huge towers or colossal blast

47. Ibid., p. 15.
48. Ibid., p. 16.

furnaces; almost everything put up without order or symmetry, just as present need dictates, mostly blackened and dirtied by coal smoke, but always giving the impression of enormous mass'.[49] It is no coincidence that gasometers are twice described as 'enormous' in this passage. For the nineteenth century, these unwieldy, massive containers came to symbolise both the amorphousness and the danger of the gas industry. Steam and gas struck the same fear into the nineteenth-century heart. Boilers and gasometers were both expected to explode at any moment.

Let us look at the report of a fairly 'ordinary' gas explosion that took place in 1862 in Paris. The *Journal für Gasbeleuchtung*, which as a professional journal, cannot be accused of exaggeration, describes the following scene:

> The café above the casino was blown up, and the two shops adjacent to the ballroom on the ground floor were totally destroyed. The heavy counter in the bar was lifted out of its moorings and flung through the air. There were casualties on the street, too, at the entrance to the casino. A woman standing in the doorway, on the pavement, was struck down dead, as if by lightning. A cart left nearby, the property of a washerwoman, was flung twenty paces by the blast. The wife of the baker across the street was badly injured, and a passerby had his nose sliced off as if by a razor blade. The gas forced its way through the passage leading to the Rue Cadet, and there exploded in a column of flame five storeys high. The blast was so powerful that people in the Rue Rochechouart at the time, 500 paces from the scene of the accident, thought that a hurricane had suddenly struck.[50]

In 1865 the measuring station of a London gas-works suffered an explosion in which ten workers lost their lives. The public was convinced that the huge gasometer, with a capacity of one million cubic feet had exploded. *The Times* considered it proven that gasometers

> are practically capable of exploding with terrible force, and that those who live near them and the buildings in their neighbourhood are

---

49. Carl Gustav Carus, *Denkwürdigkeiten aus Europa*, ed. by Manfred Schlösser (Hamburg, 1963), p. 575.

50. *Journal für Gasbeleuchtung*, 5 (1862), p. 54.

exposed to as serious consequences as if they were placed over a powder-magazine . . . at present it is clear every gasometer is a powder-magazine, and to have a gas manufactory near Westminster Abbey, St. Paul's, or one of the bridges, is much the same as if we were to store our gunpowder on the Thames Embankment.[51]

Right from the start, the gas industry was confronted with this deep-seated fear of explosions. Public attention concentrated on the gasometer, a tangible reminder of an otherwise invisible danger. In his *Historical Sketch*, William Matthews wrote:

The great increase in the number of these very capacious vessels, containing such a large quantity of gas, and their being placed in the vicinity of such a dense population, gave rise to serious considerations with respect to their safety. Besides, some explosions had occasionally happened, either from carelessness or accident; and though the mischief produced by them was comparatively trivial, yet they had of course created alarm.[52]

After the 1865 explosion in London, the *Journal of Gas Lighting, Water Supply, and Sanitary Improvement* noted that it was 'now generally admitted that gasholders will not explode, but those immense storehouses of highly inflammable gas are nevertheless looked upon suspiciously as portending some dire disaster.'[53]

Every large gas explosion fuelled the public's anxieties, and governments began to reassure their citizens. The London explosion of 1865 is a typical example. The *Journal of Gas Lighting* reported that 'in consequence of the great interest that the . . . explosion of a gasholder has excited, not only in all parts of the Kingdom, but on the Continent, Managers from the largest provincial gas-works were deputed to inspect the scene of the catastrophe, and representatives from foreign gas companies also visited the works'.[54]

From 1813 commissions were set up after every large gas

51. Quoted from *Journal of Gas Lighting, Water Supply, and Sanitary Improvement*, 14 November 1865, p. 807.
52. Matthews, *Historical Sketch*, p. 132.
53. *Journal of Gas Lighting, Water Supply, and Sanitary Improvement*, p. 808.
54. Ibid., p. 810.

explosion to establish the cause, propose improvements and allay public fears. After London's first explosion the Royal Society called together a commission of inquiry chaired by the explosives expert and chemist Sir William Congreve, well known for his experiments on rockets. The commission's report for the first time quantified the explosive power of gas, the quality that had seized the public's imagination:

> We find that the whole mechanical power of an explosion of 15,000 cubic feet of a mixture of coal gas and common air, is equal to that of the explosion of six cubic feet, or four barrels of gunpowder. . . . A more precise idea of the effects of such an explosion may be obtained from the calculation of its projectile effects, which would carry some parts of the wall of the surrounding building to a height of nearly 150 yards, and others to a distance of nearly 300. If the walls were in immediate contact with the gasometer, the height and distance would be twice as great. . . . Supposing the explosion of the gas to be unconfined, the shock would throw down a brick wall 9 feet high, and 18 inches thick, at the distance of about 50 feet from the centre; it would probably break glass windows at 150 yards.[55]

These findings led the commission to recommend that 'if Gas-lighting is to be generally introduced, the works supplying the gas should be placed at a certain distance from all other buildings; or if they are erected near houses, that reservoirs should be on a much smaller scale'.[56] In a later report, dated 1823, Congreve came to similar conclusions. When a bill to monitor the gas industry was submitted to the House of Commons, the gas industry reacted as predictably as the nuclear lobby does today. William Matthews, a spokesman for the gas industry, reported on its protest a few years later:

> The provisions of the bill were calculated to place the different gas companies completely in the power of the inspector; and, by leaving them little control over the management of their own property, very materially affected their welfare. They might be subjected to the most harassing and vexatious interruptions which either caprice, or interest, or want of adequate information, might occasion, and this without the means of redress. Besides, it was conceived, that if the

55. Quoted from Matthews, *Historical Sketch*, pp. 348–9.
56. Ibid., p. 135.

proposed enactments were passed into a law, they would probably prove a source of continual contention, and might ultimately destroy all their sanguine hopes of prosperity; for no improvement could be attempted without the consent of the inspector; and whatever knowledge, ingenuity, or industry, they might possess, must be guided by his discretion, and governed by his decisions![57]

The public's fears on the one side, the industry's obvious lack of concern on the other, and governmental supervisory bodies mediating between them — this is how the lines of battle were drawn up when the nineteenth century spawned industries that posed a potential threat to health. Positions have not changed much to the present day. The industry's employees, who generally consider public fears irrational, nevertheless may themselves suffer the consequences of an accident when equipment breaks down. An early example of the split professional personality this can give rise to is contained in the parliamentary hearing on the Congreve Commission's 1823 report. Samuel Clegg, a leading gas engineer of the day, was asked his opinion of the safety of gasometers. He replied: 'I should have no objection to my bed being placed on the top of one of them; I should sleep as sound there as in any other place.'[58] At the same hearing, Clegg described the injuries he had sustained in a gas explosion: 'The effect of it was, that it blew my hat off my head, and destroyed it, and blew it all to pieces, and knocked down two nine-inch walls, and injured me very much at the time, and burnt all the skin of my face, and the hair of my head, and I was laid up a fortnight or three weeks by it.'[59]

The Danger of Poisoning

The gasometer most clearly embodied the danger of explosion simply because of the amount of gas it contained, but it was not the only threat. Gas users far from the centre were exposed to the same danger through the existence of mains. The qualities of gas that Accum presents as especially beneficial in his *Practical*

57. Ibid., p. 151.
58. Ibid., p. 154.
59. Ibid., pp. 67–8.

Treatise on Gas-Light take on a sinister ring in this context. 'The gas', he said 'may be distributed through an infinity of ramifications of tubes with the utmost facility. . . . There is nothing to indicate its presence; no noise at the opening of the stop-cock or valve — no disturbance in the transparency of the atmosphere.'[60] Its silence, invisibility and speed were precisely the qualities that made gas seem uncanny and gas mains dangerous. Early fears concerning gas were clearly atavistic; it was believed, for example, that the pipes transmitted fire. The engineer Samuel Clegg reports that the 'the curious often applied their gloved hands to the pipes to ascertain their temperature'.[61] Even after such fears were dispelled, people tended to keep their distance. Instructions for the use of gas urged customers to turn off the main tap (the connection between the house and the gas mains) as often as possible. Blochmann suggested that 'in the interests of the occupants' safety, the tap should be kept closed when gas is not required, so that no gas can escape from the pipes'.[62] The normal time for turning off the main gas-tap was at night. While they slept, people preferred to sever all connection with such a dangerous element and restore the household's original autonomy for a few hours. Accum, an enthusiastic promoter of gas lighting, sees this precautionary measure as offering a further advantage. He presents turning off the main gas-tap as the modern equivalent of the paterfamilias locking up his house at night. 'Where gas is used, the master of the house, when he has turned the main stop-cock which conveys the gas into the collateral branch pipes, may retire to rest free from any of those apprehensions, which before harassed him, lest a candle might have been left burning, or lest the accidental dropping of a spark might become the cause of enveloping himself and family in destruction.'[63]

60. Accum, *A Practical Treatise on Gas Light . . .*, p. 100.

61. Quoted from Chandler and Lacey, *The Rise of the Gas Industry in Britain*, p. 71.

62. G.M.S. Blochmann, *Fünf Vorträge über Beleuchtung für Gasconsumenten* (Dresden, 1873), pp. 33–4. 'Turning off the main tap at night is a wise precaution; of course, this is impossible if the gas is to be on in a bedroom or nursery. But one can allow only as much gas as is needed for one or two lights to enter the pipes by positioning the tap carefully' (J.O.N. Rutter, *Das Ganze der Gasbeleuchtung, nach ihrem jetzigen Standpunkte*, Quedlinburg and Leipzig, 1835, p. 432).

63. Frederick Accum, *Description of the Process of Manufacturing Coal Gas for the Lighting of Streets, Houses, and Public Buildings . . .* (London, 1819), p. 10.

Explosions are a dramatic consequence of secretly leaking gas. But there are others, too, for gas has the additional property of being a more or less poisonous chemical. Its smell points to this side of the story. From the start, it was felt to be unpleasant, but at the same time welcomed as a useful warning. 'Its penetrating odour is a fortunate quality of gas', wrote Schilling in his manual:

> It makes gas its own best warning. A person in the waking state will rarely or never be a victim of gas poisoning. In almost all confirmed cases the accident happened at night while the victim was asleep. Generally, he had irresponsibly ignored the smell that was already clearly perceptible in the evening, and had nevertheless retired peacefully to bed. If everyone would follow the rule of never sleeping in a room in which gas can be smelled, then we would hear little of gas poisoning.[64]

Gas poisoning was soon to become a standard method of committing suicide. But apart from poisoning individuals, gas could also contaminate the soil and pollute the air. Here again gas-works were most readily identifiable as potential culprits. This consideration influenced the choice of location: 'One should try to choose a somewhat isolated site, preferably on the side where the prevailing wind blows away from the town. If there is running water, it should be used below not above the town.' To be sure, Schilling, who gives this advice, adds immediately: 'All these considerations are more a concession to the fears and prejudices of the public than strictly required by the nature of the substance.'[65]

Contamination of the soil was not limited to the immediate vicinity of the gas-works. It extended as far as the network of gas mains. Where these leaked, gas seeped into the soil. According to a report by the Medical Officer for Health in 1860, 386 million cubic feet of gas escaped into the soil in this way every year in London alone; other estimates double this figure.[66] The gas, continues the report, 'darkens the soil and makes it so offensive that the emanations from it can hardly be endured,

64. Schilling, *Handbuch für Steinkohlengas-Beleuchtung*, 3rd edn (1879).
65. Ibid., 2nd edn (1866).
66. Liberty, 'The Centenary of Gas Lighting', p. 188.

renders the basement rooms of houses uninhabitable from the
poisonous action of the gas, and even dangerous from explosions, and taints the water with filthy odours'. The gradual
poisoning of cities from underground was a nightmare that
became more and more real as the gas industry expanded:

> Gas lighting in the inner cities undoubtedly represents a more or less
> acute danger to health. Gas permeates and contaminates the subsoil
> with sulphur and ammonia. It pollutes water in wells and cisterns,
> and from leaks in the mains it escapes into the air, where it is also
> injurious to health. This lighting gas makes all excavation work
> potentially dangerous, as under certain circumstances gas can create
> conditions that promote the development of fevers, gangrenous
> rashes and a particularly virulent strain of smallpox.[67]

The Gas Flame

Gaslight, as we have said, began the industrialisation of lighting. The gas burner that replaced the oil-lamp or the candle was
no longer a lamp in the strict sense, but an extension of the
gas-works. Fears of explosion and poisoning sprang from the
uneasiness people felt at being directly connected to such a
dangerous industry. Let us look at the effects of this technical
revolution on the actual product, the flame.

The most outstanding feature of gaslight was its brightness.
The same words crop up again and again in descriptions. Gaslight was 'dazzlingly white', 'as bright as day', or 'an artificial
sun' beside which traditional sources of light paled into a weak,
reddish glow. However standardised the descriptive vocabul-
ary, when it came to establishing the intensity of the light,
claims varied widely. According to figures give by Accum, a gas
flame was three times as bright as a tallow candle,[68] while
Schilling thought it was six to ten times brighter than a wax
candle.[69] These variations are due to the pre-scientific method of
measuring light intensity in use at the time. It consisted of

67. E. Bertulus, *Memoire d'hygiène publique sur cette question: Rechercher l'influence que peut exercer l'éclairage au gaz sur la santé des masses dans l'intérieur des villes* (Marseilles, 1853), pp. 63–4.

68. Matthews, *Historical Sketch*, p. 280.

69. Schilling, *Handbuch für Steinkohlengas-Beleuchtung*, 2nd edn (1866), p. 118.

Gas flames
(Science Museum, London)

simply comparing the shadows that two lights of different brightness cast over a given distance. On this basis, one decided how much stronger or weaker they were in relation to each other. This totally subjective procedure could obviously give only approximate values.

Standards of comparison were equally inexact. There was no precisely defined and internationally recognised unit of illumination, such as was developed later — the 'standard candle', for example, which was still only a national standard, or today's units of lux and lumen. The brightness of the flames with which the gas flame was compared varied considerably, from the dim tallow candle to the relatively bright wax candle. And on top of this, flames of different sizes were often compared.

Given all these uncertainties, it is not worth trying to express light intensities precisely in figures. We shall merely say that in flames of the same size, gaslight was distinctly brighter than any other source of light known at the time. (The reason was that gas's higher temperature of combustion allowed the carbon particles that make up a flame to become white hot, while they only reached a reddish orange glow in the flames of the oil-lamp and candle.)

Higher intensity was not the only thing making gaslight bright. The larger size of its flame was also a factor. When the flame was anchored to the wick as the site of combustion, the wick determined the size and shape of the flame and the direction in which it burned. This was true of Argand's cylindrical wick and of Leger's flat wick, although they supported a much larger flame than anything else before. Only when the wick disappeared altogether did the flame become free to evolve new sizes and shapes, and to burn in directions undreamed of up till then. For example, there was no longer any law that said flames could only burn upright. Gas flames burned at an angle, sideways, and even upside down — all equally naturally. The pioneers of gas cited this unlimited potential in support of their case. Lebon, for example, the first to describe the flexibility of the gas flame, wrote: 'Soft and pure, this light may be moulded into every shape, into flowers, festoons, etc., every form suiting the flame, which may descend from a ceiling in the shape of a chalice of flowers, and spread above our heads a clear light not masked or shaded by any support whatever, darkened by no wicks, or tarnished by the least black or smoke.'[70]

We can see the eighteenth-century enthusiasm for festive illumination still at work in early gas propaganda that made much of the amusing shapes the flame could take, but in practice, a series of standard flame shapes soon evolved. They all shared a broad, flat surface, hence their names: bat-wing and fish-tail. Their shape derived from the way in which the gas issued through what was known as a 'slit burner'.[71] Compared with the illuminating surface of a candle flame, that of a gas flame was like a fully opened fan to a single segment.

Another novelty of the gas flame, apart from its brightness, was its uniformity. The light intensity of a flame burning around

70. Lebon, as in note 25. Quoted here from Hunt, *A History of the Introduction of Gas Lighting*, p. 54.

71. Another option was to have two separate flames burning at an angle to each other so that they merged to form a single, broad flame. But this is one of the technical details that we cannot pursue further here.

a wick varied enormously. 'It is never the same for two moments in succession. If there is the slightest variation in the
length of the wick, or if the wick burns down to ash — for
example, if a draught moves the flame — then the light emitted
immediately becomes brighter or dimmer.'[72] Count Rumford's
experiments showed that the luminosity of a candle decreases
from 100 to 16 within half an hour if the wick is not continually
trimmed as the process of combustion proceeds.[73] Trimming the
wick, with scissors specially adapted for the purpose, required
continuous attention, something like watching the hearth fire.
Goethe's saying, 'Wüßte nicht was sie besseres erfinden
könnten/als wenn die Lichter ohne Putzen brennten'[74] (I could
not think of a better invention than lights that burn without
needing to be trimmed) shows us how irritating people found
tending the flame around 1800. Any tasks done by candlelight
were continually interrupted. Gaslight, burning as evenly as the
gas issued from the pipe, did not require the least attention. The
only variations to which the gas flame was subject resulted from
an occasional change in the pressure under which the gas-works
sent out their product.

The third significant new feature of gaslight, after its brightness and uniformity, was that it could be regulated. Accum
points out that 'the size, shape and intensity of the gas-flame

72. A.L. Lavoisier, *Oeuvres* (Paris, 1865), Vol. 3, p. 80.
73. Gösta Bergman, *Lighting in the Theatre* (Stockholm, 1977), p. 54.
74. From 'Sprüche und Reime', Cotta edition (1855), Vol. 3, p. 13 (quoted from Otto
Hallauer, 'Beleuchtung und Auge', unpublished manuscript of the Bernoullianum Lecture,
given on 19 November 1908, p. 13).

may be regulated by simply turning a stop-cock which supplies the gas to the burner. It may at command be made to burn with an intensity sufficient to illuminate every corner of a room, or so low and dim as barely to be perceived.'[75] Or, to quote from J.W. Schmitz's *Populäres Handbuch der Gas-Beleuchtung* (1839) (Popular Manual of Gas Lighting), 'it requires only the touch of a finger to turn up the light from the tiniest spot to its dazzling full brightness'.

The ability to regulate the intensity of light was derived from Argand's wick mechanism. This had first made it possible to vary the supply of fuel and therefore the size of the flame. The advantage of the gas-tap over the wick mechanism was that lamps no longer had to be individually tended. All the lamps connected to the gas mains could be adjusted at the same time. This meant that for the first time ever, a flame could be altered from a distance. The gas-tap was the precursor of the electric switch. Technically, it was the link between the switch and the Argand burner's wick mechanism.

The technical qualities of gas lighting and its impact on perceptions can be summed up in a single word: distance. The candle and the oil-lamp were extremely intimate forms of light, as they put out only enough light to illuminate a small area. Distance, however, was inherent in gaslight from the start. Not only did its fuel come from the distant gas-works, not only could it be adjusted from a distance, without needing trimming — beyond all this, it was quite literally out of the observer's field of vision. This in turn was a consequence of its brightness. The gas flame gave out such an intense glare that people could not look at it directly. It was therefore covered with shades made of material such as frosted glass, which dissolved the concentrated core of the light. From now on, it was not the flame that glowed, but the lamp shade, which allowed an amorphous, diffuse light to filter through. (We shall have more to say about covering up the flame in the chapter 'The Drawing-room', p. 155f.). Another device also emphasised the distanced, indirect nature of gas light.

75. Accum, *A Practical Treatise on Gas-Light* . . . p. 104.

Ventilation

Candles and oil-lamps used up so little oxygen that any deterio-tation in the air was hardly noticed. Gas flames, however, which were many times larger, consumed enormous quantities of oxygen and often raised the temperature in closed rooms to tropical levels. This was gas lighting's inbuilt disadvantage. Although its brightness could be increased to almost any inten-sity, this used up so much air that it was impossible to stay in gas-lit rooms. Ventilation provided a way out of the dilemma. The classical form of ventilation consisted of replacing the air in the lighted room. A second possibility was to enclose the flame so hermetically — that is, to seal it off from the room it was lighting — that it did not draw any oxygen from the room. Lebon had already thought of such a 'distant' flame. 'The combustion of the inflammable gas', he writes,

> takes place within a glass globe supported on a tripod and cemented in such a manner as to allow none of the products to escape. The gas is conveyed in a small tube, the atmospheric air being admitted through a second tube, while a third tube leads off the products of combustion. The tube through which the air passes may draw its supply either from within or without the room, according as it is desired to renew the air in the room or not.[76]

In the nineteenth century ventilation followed this pattern. Initially, to be sure, no clear distinction was drawn between ventilating the room and enclosing the flame; they tended to be combined in one operation. An English system patented in 1817 'consisted of an arrangement of tubes, through which the pro-ducts resulting from the burning gas jets passed and by means of which a steady flow of air was taken from the interior of the room or building, and discharged to the outside'.[77] Here the connection between the gas flame and the room it illuminated was still to a large extent open.

During the second half of the nineteenth century the gas flame gradually became more hermetically separated. The ceil-ing lights, *plafond lumineux* and Sun Lights with which large

76. Quoted from Hunt, *A History of the Introduction of Gas Lighting*, p. 57.
77. Dean Chandler, *Outline of History of Lighting by Gas* (London, 1936), p. 142.

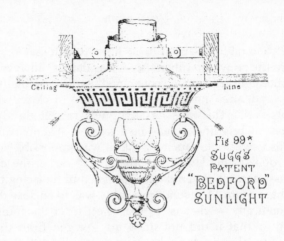

Fig 99*
SUGG'S
PATENT
"BEDFORD"
SUNLIGHT

Ventilation. In an open system, used air is removed
via the ventilating pipe above the flame (Fig. 99). In
a closed system, the flame burns in its own,
hermetically sealed combustion space (Fig. 98). The
glass casing anticipates the electric light bulb.
(*Source*: Sugg, *Domestic Lighting*.)

CLARKS PATENT
RECUPERATIVE BURNER

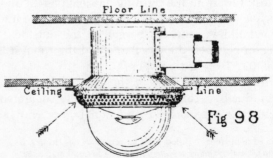

Fig 98

public rooms, theatres, parliaments, and so on, were equipped, for the first time gave gas lighting its own combustion space totally cut off from the room it was illuminating. Behind a ceiling of frosted glass, gas lighting could blaze away without regard for the quality or temperature of the air, because it had its own air supply. The number of gas jets rose correspondingly. The ceiling lighting installed in the Théatre de la Gaité in Paris in 1862 consisted of 1,338 individual gas jets.[78] Without the glass encasing it, this sea of flames would have roasted the audience. The French term *plafond lumineux* is most appropriate because the many flames which made up the ceiling illumination did not appear as individual entities, but created a single, large surface of light. It gradually replaced the chandelier which, with its many individual lights, was a magnificent example of 'close' light: each flame functioned both on its own and as a part of the whole. The chandelier therefore never lost the intimacy of the single flame. Remembering this sort of light, Charles Garnier, the architect of the Paris Opera, commented on the light of the *plafond lumineux*:

One feels enclosed, hemmed in by an enormous circle of fire, a sort of magnified, oppressive lens, whose rays of light seem threatening. The room is bright, really very bright indeed, but it has nothing cheerful about it. It is the false light of dawn mingling with the candlelight of a ballroom. A wonderful advantage of artificial illumination is lost: the sight of the light itself. It by far surpasses the sight of *caged* and reflected light, which gives the impression of a luridly glowing furnace, instead of the flickering light of a real fire [emphasis added].[79]

The End of the Flame: Incandescent Gaslight

In the *plafond lumineux* gas lighting had been taken as far as it could go. But before it was replaced by more efficient electric light, it made a surprising comeback in a different form.

---

78. Carl-Friedrich Baumann, 'Entwicklung und Anwendung der Bühnenbeleuchtung seit der Mitte des achtzehnten Jahrhunderts' (unpublished dissertation, University of Cologne, 1956), pp. 148–9.
79. Quoted from ibid., pp. 150–1.

In 1886 the Austrian chemist and engineer Auer von Wels-bach invented incandescent gaslight, which exploited the power of the flame to heat rather than to illuminate. Incandescent gaslight was produced by heating an incandescent mantle, made of a suitable alloy (rare earth), in a Bunsen flame until it reached white heat. The light it gave out was several times brighter than traditional gaslight and used less gas to produce. Thus the flame was dethroned as the source of light. Reduced to the flame of Bunsen and no longer visible, it functioned only indirectly by giving off heat. This innovation made gaslight with an open flame obsolète at a single stroke. It even posed a serious threat to electric light, as it only cost one-fifth to one-sixth as much to produce.[80]

'It is electric light without electricity.'[81] This succinct defini-tion of incandescent gas lighting, given in 1887, reveals the source of its inspiration. It was the result of an attempt by the older gas technology to survive by mimicking the more recent, promising technology — and it was successful for some time. Gas lighting could draw on a development that had taken place in its own history. Long before Auer von Welsbach constructed the incan-descent mantle, the technical principle was known. Drum-mond's 'limelight', which had been used to achieve special lighting effects on the stage since about 1830, consisted of a piece of lime that was heated by a hydrogen flame until it glowed, emitting an intense light. But gas lighting needed the successful example of electric indandescent light to push it onto this path. Arc lighting and the electric bulb demonstrated that heating solid bodies produced a brighter, more even light more cheaply than did an open flame. This was the spur to imitate with gas what had been achieved with electricity. There are other examples of this technical mimicry. Electrical technology clearly inspired the gas switches developed around 1900. The old gas-taps merely regulated the size of the flame via the supply of gas, and required a constant pilot light. The new mechanisms, by contrast, were true switches, which could turn

---

80. Hans-Joachim Braun, 'Gas oder Elektrizität? Zur Konkurrenz zweier Beleuchtungssy-steme, 1880–1914', *Technikgeschichte*, vol. 47, no. 1 (1980).

81. *Financial Times*, 21 March 1887, quoted from Chandler, *Outline of History of Lighting by Gas*, p. 193.

the incandescent mantle on and off at a distance, like an electric light.[82]

Here we have stumbled on a new theme: the impact of newly √ created technologies on old ones. This is the other, complementary side of technical progress. So far we have followed the history of artificial illumination as a simple straight line. Lighting technology appears to have progressed in logical steps from the hearth flame via the torch, the candle and the Argand lamp to gaslight, without faltering or looking back. But technical progress is more than a resolute stride forward; it also involves the developmental stages that have been left behind. Often, these do not simply disappear, but live on, in modified — that is, modernised — form. Nathan Rosenberg, an American economic historian, describes several instances of old technologies that were modernised in this way. From this he derives the theory that 'the "old" technology continues to be improved after the introduction of the "new", thus postponing even further the time when the old technology is clearly outmoded'.[83] One example he cites is the changes in sailing ship construction that took place in the nineteenth century in response to the development of the steam ship. Sailing ships were 'old' technology but were modernised to such an extent that for a considerable time they seriously rivalled steam shipping.

The history of illumination offers several cases of old technologies modernising in the wake of new developments. The candle is a good example. Soon after gaslight had made the wick redundant, thus doing away with the necessity for trimming it, candlewicks were developed that no longer needed trimming either. Gas technology, too, produced the synthetic fuel paraffin as a by-product of coal distillation. Paraffin burnt more cleanly and brightly than the organic materials wax and tallow, and was cheaper to produce. These improvements allowed the candle to maintain its position as a source of light, at least in areas where gas and electricity did not gain immediate access. The petroleum lamp, finally, was the most significant example of this sort of

---

82. Patent application by Conrad Adolf Weber-Marti, Zurich, 1889 (Chandler, *Outline of History of Lighting by Gas*, p. 229).

83. Braun, 'Gas oder Elektrizität?' p. 1 (Nathan Rosenberg, 'Factors Affecting the Diffusion of Technology', *Explorations in Economic History*, formerly *Explorations in Entrepreneurial History*, vol. 10, no. 1, Fall, 1972, pp. 3–33, quotation on p. 23).

modernisation. Technically, it was nothing but an Argand burner. But the 'modern' fuel it used increased its illuminating
power to such an extent that for a long time it was competitive
with gas and even electric light.

In all these cases the old technology was infiltrated, as it were,
by elements of a new technology. While the old technical principle was retained, new materials and processes did the work of
modernisation. As always when new wine is filled into old
bottles, however, the victory of the new technology could not be
put off for ever.

Electrical Apotheosis

> The sunlight poured upon the rank
> vegetation of the carboniferous forests, was
> gathered and stored up, and has been waiting
> through the ages to be converted again into
> light. The latent force accumulated during the
> primeval days, and garnered up in the coal
> beds, is converted, after passing in the
> steam-engine through the phases of chemical,
> molecular and mechanical force, into
> electricity, which only waits the touch of the
> inventor's genius to flash out into a million
> domestic suns to illuminate a myriad homes.
> (Francis R. Upton, 1880)

Gaslight seemed to be the lighting of infinite possibility, so long
as its brightness could be increased easily and at will. But it soon
became apparent that there was a catch — gaslight consumed
enormous amounts of oxygen. Up to a certain point, of course,
ventilation could replace the air used up and heated by the ever
larger and ever more numerous gas flames. But in the long run it
was obvious that gas lighting had struck a natural barrier. This
first became clear in the theatre — the place with the greatest
appetite for light in the nineteenth century. Visiting the theatre
often gave people headaches, not because of the performance
but because of the air: 'We all of us know that the times when
we suffer most from the effect of artificial light is in crowded

places of public amusement, which are at the same time brilliantly lighted. Many of us are unable to go to the theatre or to
attend evening performances of any kind, as the intense head-
ache which invariably attends or follows our stay in such places
entirely prevents them.'[84] During a night at the theatre, the
temperature measured under the ceiling of the auditorium could
rise from 60 °F to 100 °F (15 °C to 38 °C).[85] While the increase
was less extreme in the stalls and lower balconies, it remained
uncomfortable enough. Private houses suffered similar conditions: 'When we take the library ladder to get a book from the
upper shelf we find our head and shoulders plunged in a
temperature like that of a furnace, producing giddiness and
general malaise.'[86]

The deterioration in the quality of the air not only caused
headaches and sweating, it also had an unpleasant effect on the
interior decoration of rooms. As it burned, gas gave off small
quantities of ammonia and sulphur, as well as carbon dioxide
and water. At the beginning of the nineteenth century, gaslight
had been celebrated as cleanliness and purity incarnate. Seventy
years later the same gaslight seemed dirty and unhygienic —
something that would inexorably destroy the most beautiful
decorations:

> Everyone is familiar with the luxuriousness of public rooms, which
> vie with each other in opulence and elegance in order to make a visit
> there comfortable. Paintings, sculpture and architecture compete
> with fantastic and graceful figures and allegories in embellishing
> walls, friezes and ceilings. . . . Some time later, however, the gas
> flames began their work of destruction. They blackened the ceilings
> and marked joins in the gilding; most surfaces turned yellow and oil
> paintings almost disappeared or were darkened by smoke.[87]

> The discolouration or darkening of paintings and the dulling of metal
> decorations an also be attributed to the effects of the combustion
> products of gas.[88]

84. R.E.B. Crompton, *Artificial Lighting in Relation to Health, A Paper Read at Conference Held
at the International Health Exhibition, South Kensington* (London, n.d. [1881]), p. 9.

85. Ibid., p. 7.

86. Ibid., p. 6.

87. *L'Evénement*, 23 October 1881, quoted from *Das Edisonlicht. Elektrisches Beleuchtungssys-
tem* (Berlin, 1882), pp. 62–3.

88. Alfred von Urbanitzky, *Die elektrischen Beleuchtungsanlagen* (Vienna/Pest/Leipzig,
1883), p. 119.

Where gaslight failed, electric light took over, repeating at a
higher technical level what gaslight had achieved in its time.
Gaslight represented progress over candles and oil-lamps in that
it did away with the wick; electric light went one step further
and abolished the flame. Electric light did not use up oxygen,
and left the chemical composition of the air unchanged. Unlike
gaslight, it could really be intensified at will.

Before these qualities were perfected in the electric light bulb,
electrical technology bred a hybrid which provides another
illustration of how gradually technology changes. The transition
from an open gas flame to the closed electric bulb was made by
open electrical incandescent lighting.

Arc Lighting

The pioneer of electro-chemistry, Humphry Davy, was the first
to observe the light produced by a discharge of electric current
between two carbon electrodes. This took place in 1800, and
here is how he described the phenomenon twelve years later:
'When pieces of charcoal, about an inch long and one-sixth of an
inch in diameter, were brought near each other (within the
thirtieth or fortieth part of an inch), a bright spark was
produced . . . , and by which drawing the points from each
other a constant discharge took place through the heated air, in
a space at least equal to four inches, producing a most brilliant
ascending arch of light.'[89]

Arc lighting, as it has been called since Davy, is not produced
primarily by the electric arc itself, as was first assumed. It is
caused mainly by the electric charge heating the carbon electrodes to white heat. In this respect, arc lighting is in fact
incandescent lighting. At the same time, however, it is also
produced by combustion, as the carbon particles actually smoul-
der in the surrounding air. Unlike incandescent light enclosed in

89. Humphry Davy, *Elements of Chemical Philosophy* (London, 1812), Vol. 1, p. 152. Davy,
incidentally, was not the only person to produce an 'arch of light' at that time. During the
first ten years of the nineteenth century many researchers were conducting experiments
with the voltaic pile, in the course of which they observed the discharge of an arc of light
(Walter Biegon von Czudnochowski, *Das elektrische Bogenlicht. Seine Entwicklung und seine
physikalischen Grundlagen*, Leipzig, 1904, pp. 4ff).

Jablochkov Candle.
A form of electric arc lighting in general use in the 1870s, featuring
a peculiar combination of old and new technology. The two carbon
rods were separated by an insulating layer of gypsum and, when
the electric arc had been 'lit', burned down in about one and a half
hours.
(*Source*: A. Bernstein, *Die elektrische Beleuchtung*, Berlin, 1880.)

an airtight container, open arc lighting 'burns' at the electrodes,
consuming them as the candle flame consumes the wax shaft.
An arc lighting installation in general use in the 1870s functioned quite literally in this way. In the Jablochkov Candle,
named after its Russian inventor, the electrodes took the form of
two parallel carbon rods separated by an insulating layer of
gypsum. The top was lit and the candle burned down slowly
until the carbon rods were consumed, whereupon the light
went out, as in the traditional candle. Placing the electrodes in a
vacuum put an end to this electric combustion. In the closed
arc-lamp, they were hermetically sealed in glass. The only way
in which the arc lamp differed from later incandescent lighting
was that the light emanated from white hot electrodes rather
than from a filament.

It took a surprisingly long time for more general applications to be found for arc lighting. More than forty years passed before it was used outside the laboratory and even then it was used only sporadically — for special effects in the theatre, or large-scale festive illuminations. Not until 1870 was it firmly enough established to become part of the general lighting scene.

Initially, development was slow because of purely technical factors. Arc lighting as Davy developed it had no practical uses until three prerequisites were met. Firstly, a mechanism was needed to keep the gap between the electrodes equal as they burned down. The first regulators that did this job were constructed in the 1840s; the problem was finally solved in 1878 when Hefner-Alteneck, who worked with Siemens, developed the differential regulator.

Secondly, the electricity supply had to be improved. Volta's battery, although much improved after 1830 by Danniell, Grove and Bunsen, could not cope in the long term. The dynamos constructed by Gramme and Siemens in 1867 made it possible for the first time to produce large amounts of electricity continuously.

Thirdly, the electrodes had to be made of better material. Simple charcoal, which Davy used, burned too irregularly and, above all, too quickly. The synthetic carbon rods in use from 1840 smouldered very slowly and emitted a bright, even light.

As a result of these technical improvements, arc lighting was fully operational by the 1870s. But in practice, its use was limited to factories, shops, railway stations, building sites, wharves and so on — in short, to large spaces with an insatiable appetite for light. It was simply too intense for use in other places, such as houses. Arc lighting was the first artificial source that produced too much light for many purposes. Unlike all earlier innovations in lighting which had been metaphorically compared to the sun, arc lighting really did resemble sunlight, as spectrum analysis shows. As bright as daylight, arc-light overwhelmed people when they experienced it for the first time. It was as though the sun had suddenly risen in the middle of the night. In 1855 the engineers Lacassagne and Thiers staged an experiment with their arc lighting system in Lyon. The *Gazette de France* reported the event in the following terms:

Arc lighting in the Place de la Concorde (1844).
'The light, which flooded a large area, was so strong that ladies opened up
their umbrellas — not as a tribute to the inventors, but in order to protect
themselves from the rays of this mysterious new sun' (newspaper report).
(*Source: La Lumière électrique*, 1883)

Strollers out near the Chateau Beaujou yesterday evening at about 9
p.m. suddenly found themselves bathed in a flood of light that was
as bright as the sun. One could in fact have believed that the sun had
risen. This illusion was so strong that birds, woken out of their sleep,
began singing in the artificial daylight. . . . The light, which flooded
a large area, was so strong that ladies opened up their umbrellas —
not as a tribute to the inventors, but in order to protect themselves
from the rays of this mysterious new sun.[90]

Arc-light was measured in thousands of candle powers,
whereas gaslight was at best reckoned in dozens. Concentrated
in a floodlight, arc-light could light up military targets at distances of up to six kilometres. Next to its intensity, its absolute

90. J. Lacassagne and R. Thiers, *Nouveau système d'éclairage électrique* (Paris and Lyon,
1857), p. 25.

Large building-site under arc-lights.
(*Source*: Fontaine, *Éclairage à l'électricité*)

steadiness was the most striking thing about arc lighting. The *Gazette de Lyon* wrote about Lacassagne's and Thiers' experiment: 'Like everyone else we, too, were surprised by the brightness of this light. The thing that impressed us most, however, was its evenness, its unchanging quality, its absolute steadiness.'[91]

Though these qualities undoubtedly made arc lighting the most modern form of illumination of its day, it was a technological step backwards from gaslight. Arc-light was, in nineteenth-century terminology, indivisible; that is, its intensity could not be varied. Nor was there a central supply system that could serve many lights at once. Every arc light had its own separate battery. Like the candle and the oil lamp, arc lighting was governed by the pre-industrial principle of a self-sufficient supply.

91. 19 June 1855, quoted from ibid., p. 19.

Arc lighting and the colonial wars (1884).
'When the rebels were only a few hundred metres away and had begun to attack, the electric floodlights suddenly blazed into action, bathing them in the most brilliant light. The surprise and confusion were so complete that they defy description' (report on the use of arc lighting in the Sudan).
(*Source*: *La Lumière électrique*, 1884.)

Before electric light could serve as a general source of illumination suitable also for use in private houses, these disadvantage of arc lighting had to be overcome. The next move was obviously to appropriate the technical achievements of gas lighting — its adjustability and central supply — in a reversal of the process, described above, by which old technologies imitate new ones. On closer inspection, Edison's incandescent electric light is, in fact, nothing but a methodical imitation of gaslight in a new medium.

The Electric Bulb

Edison's 1879 experiment with incandescent electricity, lasting more than forty hours, was not the world's first glimpse of this type of lighting. During his experiments early in the nineteenth century, Davy had already observed that a wire — in this case platinum — carrying an electric current heats up evenly and eventually begins to glow. Nor did Edison discover that placing the wire in a vacuum prevented it from burning away. Frederick De Moleyn, an Englishman, had achieved this in 1841. And finally, the trial that Heinrich Göbel, an American inventor of German descent, conducted against Edison established that the carbon filament lamp Göbel had constructed as early as in the 1850s 'had been a truly serviceable source of light, and that Göbel had thus been using a practical incandescent lamp, and had shown it in public, twenty or thirty years before Edison'.[92]

Edison is important not because of an isolated invention but because he perfected existing elements and combined them in an operational technical unit. He also had a great gift for publicity. (In this respect, he can be compared to Winsor, the pioneer of gas lighting. On the other hand, Edison's great technical gift separates him from Winsor.)

Edison began his work on the technology of lighting with the declared aim of producing an incandescent light that shared all the advantages of gaslight without using up the air. His notebooks contain the following entries: 'Edison's great effort — not to make a large light or blinding light, but a small light having the mildness of gas'; 'Object, Edison to effect exact imitation of all done by gas, so as to replace lighting by gas by lighting by electricity.'[93]

Edison's carbon filament lamp, put together in 1879 and made public at the Paris Electricity Exposition two years later, was instantly hailed as a successful imitation of gaslight. For the first time, progress was made not by increasing the intensity of light but by imitating existing levels using new technology. An advertising brochure issued by Edison states that 'the light given out by the lamp resembles gaslight in colour and intensity, but

92. Artur Fürst, *Das elektrische Licht* (Munich, 1926), p. 124.
93. George S. Bryan, *Edison: The Man and His Work* (London and New York, 1926), p. 111.

Early electric light bulbs and filaments.
Initially, the only way to make electric light brighter was to increase the number of filaments. The imagination was totally free to devise interesting shapes for filaments and bulbs. Can we see this playfulness as an attempt to compensate for the uniformity of electric light?
(*Source*: *La Lumière électrique*, 1881, 1886)

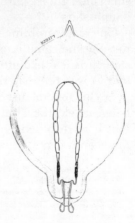

differs from it in that it is absolutely even and steady'.[94] All independent observers confirmed this claim. For example, a French report of the 1881 Paris Electricity Exposition made the following points:

> We normally imagine electric light to be a blindingly bright light, whose harshness hurts the eyes. . . . Here, however, we have a light source that has somehow been civilised and adapted to our needs. Every individual light shines like gaslight, but this is a type of gas that has not yet been invented — a gas that gives a completely steady light but nevertheless shines vividly and brightly and places no strain on the retina. But then — how different from gas! Electric light leaves no combustion residues in the house — no carbon dioxide and carbon monoxide to pollute the air, no sulphuric acid and ammonia to damage paintings and fabrics. Electricity does not raise the air temperature, and does not give off the uncomfortable and fatiguing warmth associated with gas lighting. It puts an end to the danger of explosion or fire. It is not affected by fluctuations in the outside temperature or changes in mains pressure. . . . It shines evenly and steadily, irrespective of the season . . . and in water as well as in air. It is totally independent of all external influences.[95]

The popular magazine *Die Gartenlaube* carried a report of the Exposition listing the same qualities, and saw the electric light bulb quite literally as a reduced version of the arc-light: 'There is no flickering and not the slightest noise; drawing rooms are not heated up — there is only the most extraordinarily pleasant, pure air; added to this is the comfortable, lively colour of the small arc-light [*sic*]: truly, this must be almost the "ideal form of illumination".'[96]

One factor in bringing the light of the early electric bulbs to roughly the same intensity and quality as gaslight (by today's standards it was a little weaker than that of a twenty-five watt bulb[97]) was the material used for the filament. The *carbon* filament in general use until the late 1890s represented a link between electric light and older lighting technologies, all of which were based on the combustion of carbon rods. In the nineteenth-century psychology of light, it was important to

94. *Das Edisonlicht*, p. 14.
95. Henry de Parville, *L'Electricité et ses applications*, 2nd edn (Paris, 1883) pp. 354–5.
96. Quoted from *Das Edisonlicht*, p. 71.
97. Terence Rees, *Theatre Lighting in the Age of Gas* (London, 1978), p. 171.

establish this continuity, as it allowed people to see the old in the new, and thus the new as something familiar. 'Since . . . the luminosity of the coal gas flame is due to incandescing particles of carbon set free in the flame, and which are subsequently burnt up, and the light of the electric incandescent lamp consists of incandescent rays emitted by the carbon filament which is heated by the electric current, it follows that the nature and character of the light from both are the same.'[98]

In quality, gaslight and electric light were almost interchangeable, but an examination of the light source itself soon revealed the differences between them. The filament's surface was only a fraction of the size of a flame; it therefore had to glow much more brightly in order to cast the same amount of light. Everyday perceptions, still geared towards the gas flame, had to be trained to see the filament at all. 'Born and educated in the use of illuminants which present to the eye a soft wide gaseous flame, having a measurable irridescent surface containing incandescent particles widely dispersed, we were quite unprepared to estimate the increased power of the brilliant little line of intense incandescence that meets our view when we regard this glow lamp.'[99]

We will describe the impact which the substitution of filament for flame had on perceptions in a later chapter ('The Drawing-room', p. 167f.). In the meantime, looking at the filament's progress allows us to follow the physical microstructure of the modernisation process. The eye would have to come to terms with its results.

With filaments made of carbonised plant fibres, the electric bulb had an organic basis. The structure of the fibres determined the quality of the light that was produced. A description dating from 1890 of the process by which electric bulbs were manufactured points out how important it is that 'the structure of the wood [sic] has not been destroyed by fungi or rot. In one case a factory could not turn out a single good lamp for a whole week because it had been supplied with rotten bamboo from China.'[100] The structure of the carbonised paper that Edison had

98. *Lancet*, vol. 1 (1895), p. 52.

99. *Electrical Engineer*, December 1886, p. 261.

100. J. Zacharias, *Die Glühlampe, ihre Herstellung und Anwendung in der Praxis* (Vienna, Pest and Leipzig, 1890), pp. 18–19.

From bamboo to filament.
The illustration shows the gradual
transformation of nature into technology.
The particular bamboo that, after many years
of searching, Edison had selected as the most
suitable for his purpose was split repeatedly
to separate it into fine fibres, which were
carbonised and then bent into the shape of a
filament.
(*Source: L'Electricité*, 1882)

used in his first experiments proved to be unsuitable:

The very short fibres that make up paper are arranged in many irregular layers. The current therefore cannot find an even path through the filament, but has constantly to surmount changing obstacles. There are also countless spots where the current can only continue on its way by crossing very narrow air pockets embedded in the structure of the paper, with the result that extremely fine sparks are created. These contribute to the rapid disintengration of the filament.[101]

Looking for a suitable fibre, Edison carbonised almost 6,000 vegetable substances. He started with everyday materials such as paper, yarn, cork, celluloid, linen, wood, and human and animal hair,[102] and discovered that bamboo fibre was particularly well suited to his purpose. An international search for the optimal bamboo fibre followed, in the course of which Edison's assistants combed the jungles of South America and the wastelands of China. Eventually, they discovered a species of bamboo with especially long and regular fibres in Japan. Edison concluded a supply agreement with a Japanese planter, and thus was created a bamboo plantation whose sole purpose was to cultivate material for the production of filaments.[103]

This step represents the peak of the rationalisation of organic fibre. It was succeeded by the fibreless, synthetic filament, whose production involved a completely new process. The material used first was cellulose which, 'in the form of a quick-setting paste, was forced through nozzles to produce an endless thread of absolutely regular diameter. It was wound on to a spool and then cut into the required lengths.'[104] The metal alloys that followed a little later were produced by the same method. In a further example of the interaction between old and new technologies, the first practical metal filament lamp — the osmium lamp — was constructed in 1898 by Auer von Welsbach, who a few years earlier had so successfully 'transferred' the technology of electric incandescent lighting to gas in creating incandescent gaslight. The knowledge of materials that he developed in the process, or rather, that made his discovery possible in the first place, now proved amenable to a 'counter-transference' back to electric light, completing the circle of mutual influence.

In the 1890s all sorts of metal alloys were used for filaments, each one producing a brighter light than the last. This is how the

101. Fürst, *Das elektrische Licht*, p. 95.
102. Bryan, *Edison*, p. 127.
103. Ibid., pp. 133–4.
104. Fürst, *Das elektrische Licht*, p. 128.

electric light industry tried to combat the competition of gas incandescent lighting. Eventually, just before the First World War, the tungsten filament was developed. This perfected incandescent lighting, which finally realised its full range, from a weak reddish glow right through to the blinding white light of a modern 300-watt light bulb. Edison's carbon filament lamp belonged to the nineteenth century because it was no brighter than a gas flame. The tungsten lamp, however, betrayed no hint of this origin. Twentieth-century illumination had begun.

Electrification

Light intensity and quality were not the only ways in which the Edison lamp copied gaslight. In other essential aspects, too, it was modelled on its predecessor — most significantly in the transferral of the idea of a central supply. Arc lighting had been able to dispense with this as it was suitable only for large public rooms and spaces, which could accommodate their own generators without difficulty. This situation changed the moment the electric bulb turned electric light into a form of illumination that could be used everywhere. As it was impractical to provide a generator for every private house, a central supply modelled on the gas supply was an obvious solution. In 1880, when the electric bulb was available but a central supply of electricity was not, the situation was described as follows:

> We city dwellers can have gas supplied to our house, ready for use. We turn on a tap, hold a lighted match to the mouth of the pipe and that is the end of our efforts to obtain a light. We turn off the tap and the light goes out. This is extremely convenient — one is tempted to say, seductively convenient. Electric light is a different matter; we have to generate our own electricity, as there is no company yet that supplies it.[105]

Edison developed the central electricity station on the model of the gas-works just as seventy years earlier Winsor had conceived a central gas supply along the lines of the water supply.

---

105. Alex Bernstein, *Die elektrische Beleuchtung* (Berlin, 1880), p. 61.

Edison's dynamo (1881).
(*Source*: A. Fürst, *Das elektrische Licht*, 1926)

The first central electricity stations became operational in 1882 in London and New York. A French writer, describing them one year later for readers who were unfamiliar with the subject, presents them as electrified gas-works:

> The gas supply, which on the basis of long experience offers itself as a model, functions as follows: one or more gas-works are built in every city, according to the size of the area to be supplied. Correspondingly, the American inventor [Edison] plans to set up one or more electricity generating stations, according to the size of the area. Gas is conveyed underground through large pipes, which follow the main transport routes; from this network of mains, smaller pipes lead off into the side streets, and even smaller supply pipes branch off from these, taking the gas into individual houses. This type of supply system has been adopted for the distribution of electricity. Mains go out from every central electricity station, these branch out into secondary cables and from these in turn supply cables lead off to individual houses. Electric cables resemble gas pipes except that they have a much smaller diameter. The largest is no thicker than an arm.[106]

106. de Parville, *L'Electricité*, pp. 375–6.

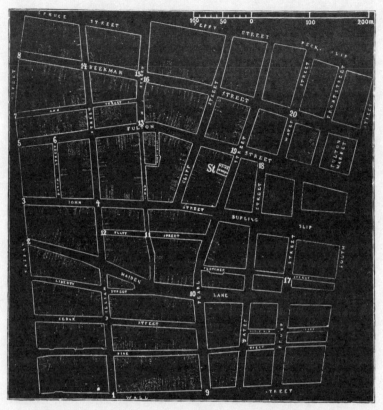

Area supplied by the first central electricity station, New York, 1883.
Consumers are shown as bright dots; the location of the station is indicated
by the letters 'St'.
(*Source*: Fürst, *Das elektrische Licht*)

Of course, the days of electricity imitating the gas supply were
numbered. When it became apparent that high-voltage current
could be transported over long distances without an appreciable
loss of voltage, it took only a few years to develop a new system
that evoked no memories of gas-works. Central electricity stations were replaced by power stations built not in the cities they
supplied but in areas where the energy required to generate
electricity was cheapest. The new locations — in coal-mining
districts, near waterfalls or dams — were often hundreds of
kilometres away from where the electricity was used. (The first

significant overhead transmission line, which became operational in 1891 and linked a power station at Lauffen on the Neckar with Frankfurt on Main, was 179 kilometres long.) Modern, high-capacity power stations no longer supply a single town, but a whole region. The consequences of this centralisation are most obvious when the electricity supply fails. A blackout paralyses a whole region as quickly as the prick of a spindle sends the whole palace to sleep in the fairy tale of the Sleeping Beauty. As with the method of electricity supply, the first electric light switches were also modelled on gas lighting. 'Every arm of a chandelier and every lamp has a revolving switch, reminiscent of a gas tap. When it is operated, the electrical circuit between the bulb and the underground cable is closed and the light burns. The opposite action breaks the circuit and the light goes out. If the house has no electricity, there is no light either.'[107] The electric *switch* is progress over the gas-*tap* in that it is turned on and off in one movement. Unlike gaslight that had to be physically lit — 'One turns on the tap, lights a match and the light flares up'[108] — and then began to burn with the leisureliness of a candle flame, electric light comes on in an instant: 'You come home, turn on the switch, and without fire, without a match, the whole house lights up.'[109] The novelty of switches stimulated people's imagination; as we can see, in the above example it is not simply one room, but the whole house that is suddenly bathed in light. And the author immediately goes on to describe a lighting system that switches itself on and off automatically: 'Is it too much trouble to press a button or operate a revolving switch? Well then, you open the door of your hall, and the light goes on by itself. You enter the living room, and the lights are on. . . . Similarly, the light turns itself on automatically when you enter the bedroom or the study. Simply by opening a door, you cause the light to come on in the room.'[110]

For obvious reasons, this vision never became reality. What eventually happened was that the light switch was placed next to the door, allowing people to choose whether they wanted to

107. Ibid.
108. Ibid., p. 355.
109. Ibid.
110. Ibid., pp. 355–6.

Early light switches. The light switch's origins in the gas-tap remained
clearly visible for many years. Early electric switches were *turned*, and they
were placed on each individual light. Actual switches and the ability to turn
lights on at a distance are much later developments.
(*Source*: A. Fürst in *La Lumière électrique*)

enter a room in darkness or in light. (This naturally also had the advantage that the door of a room could be shut without the light turning itself off automatically.)

The fact that electric light could be switched on and off instantly was recognised as a fundamentally new property compared with gaslight. Nevertheless, the earliest form of electric switch, the *revolving switch*, was nothing but an imitation of a gas-tap: contact was established *gradually*, as though it were a matter of regulating a gas supply, not closing an electrical circuit. The revolving switch was unsuitable for electricity because, as was discovered retrospectively, in 1926, 'it switched off the current too slowly — not instantly through spring action. Disconnection was determined by the speed with which the switch was turned.'[111]

The examples of a central electricity supply and the light switch show how varied the results can be when a new technology borrows from an older one. While the central electricity station modelled on the gas-works perfected electrical technology, the revolving switch, an imitation of the gas-tap, was a backwards step. As this chapter has shown, the interplay of mimicry between old and new technologies is riddled with such contradictory results. But in the end, developmental mistakes are always corrected. The electrical revolving switch, for example, was soon replaced by the spring action quick-break switch which is still used for electric lights today.

The enthusiasm with which electric light was hailed in the late nineteenth century is in many respects reminiscent of the reaction evoked by gas lighting seventy years earlier. In their time, both innovations were regarded as the most modern, the brightest, cleanest and most economical form of lighting; in both cases, their industrial nature was obvious; and finally, electric light seemed to be nothing other than an imitation of the system of gas lighting.

There were, however, also important differences between them. While the bourgeois household was reluctant to admit gas because of its unpleasant smell and its poisonous, explosive

---

111. Fürst, *Das elektrische Licht*, p. 102.

Electricity and health: electrification.
(*Source*: *L'Electricité*, 1882)

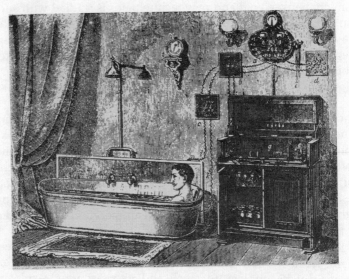

Electricity and health: an electric bath.
(*Source*: *L'Electricité*, 1882)

nature, all doors were immediately opened to electric light: 'The Edison light is penetrating not only into rooms that are at present lit by gas, but even into those that are closed to it — that is, elegant apartments and drawing-rooms — and replacing candles in chandeliers and candelabra.'[112] It was electricity's properties as a pure, odourless and non-physical form of energy that made it immediately acceptable in drawing-rooms. Electricity did not endanger life or health; on the contrary, it was regarded as positively beneficial, almost as a sort of vitamin. For the century of Hermann von Helmholtz, electricity, energy and life were synonymous. Electricity was believed to be, and was used as, a means of restoring exhausted energies. In a study of the late-nineteenth-century obsession with exhaustion, we read that 'in the chemical and technological warfare against fatigue one weapon stands out among the rest: electricity. If fatigue was the disorder of energy, electricity held out the promise of restitution.'[113] In agriculture, electrictity was used like a fertiliser. 'Electro-culture' consisted of 'galvanising' the land that was to be cultivated. Radishes and carrots that had been treated in this way 'had an exquisite flavour and were very tender and juicy', as a description of such experiments in the 1890s tells us.'The average yield of "galvanised" plants compared with those grown in the normal way is 4 : 1 for vegetables and root crops, and 3 : 2 for other crops.'[114] Medicine had been fascinated by electricity and magnetism since the end of the eighteenth century. Now it began to use available electrical technology to treat the body rather like 'electro-culture' was treating the soil. The spectrum of electro-therapy ranged from continuous galvanic current to electric-shock treatment.[115] A French patent application, made in 1882 and entitled 'Mode d'application de l'électricité, pour les vêtements, sur le corps humaine', proposed the following method of exposing the body to electricity: 'Two pockets, sewn on to the sides of the garment, each contain

112. *Journal des débats*, quoted from *Das Edisonlicht*, p. 59.

113. Anson Rabinbach, 'The Age of Exhaustion: Energy and Fatigue in the late 19th century' (unpublished manuscript), p. 38. (French translation published as 'L'Àge de la fatigue; énergie et fatigue à la fin du 19e siècle', *Urbi*, no. 2, December 1979, p. 46).

114. Alfred Ritter von Urbanitzky, *Die Elektrizität im Dienste der Menschheit* (Vienna, Pest and Leipzig, 1895), p. 353.

115. See George Beard, *Medical and Surgical Uses Of Electricity* (1874); see also Rabinbach manuscript, p. 39.

Electric jewels.
(*Source*: *L'Illustration*, 1881)

The Palace of Electricity at the Paris Exposition of 1900:
exterior view.
(Archiv für Kunst und Geschichte, Berlin)

a small battery. Two vertical metal bands are attached to the batteries, and from the bands, metal wires go out to all parts of the body. In order to allow electricity to flow through the body, the inventor has fastened small metal plates to the wires at certain intervals. These plates lie on the skin.'[116]

The practical applications of electricity were not limited to medicine, agriculture and illumination. Between 1880 and 1920 electricity began to permeate modern, urban life. Local traffic systems, lifts, the telephone, radio and cinema as well as a constantly growing number of household appliances would have been inconceivable without electricity. Electrical energy had the same impact on material culture as on the body. Ac-

---

116. Quoted from *La Lumière électrique*, vol. 9 (1883), p. 252. This type of electro-therapy naturally reminds us of the use of electricity as a means of execution. When the electric chair was first used in the United States in 1890, it was justified in terms of the scientific precision, painlessness and so on of death by electrocution. The French journal *Electricité* commented: 'La connaissance de la manière dont l'électricité donne la mort n'est-elle point indispensable pour savoir comment elle peut être utilisée à entretenir la vie?' (*Electicité*, 1890, p. 448).

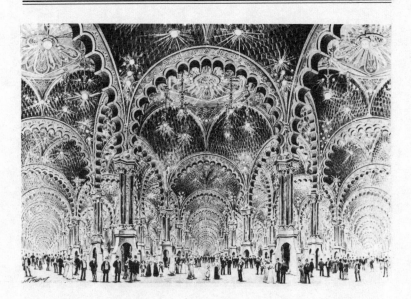

The Palace of Electricity: interior view.

cording to the *Scientific American* supplement of 7 March 1900, the general public believed that if there was anything under the sun that electricity could not do, then it was not worth doing.[117]

The period of electrification also witnessed changes in the economic structure of capitalism. The transformation of free competition into corporate monopoly capitalism confirmed in economic terms what electrification had anticipated technically: the end of individual enterprise and an autonomous energy supply. It is well known that the electrical industry was a significant factor in bringing about these changes. An analogy between electrical power and finance capital springs to mind. The concentration and centralisation of energy in high-capacity power stations corresponded to the concentration of economic power in the big banks. Werner Sombart wrote: 'Production and distribution, trade and commerce are becoming more and more dependent on banks and stock exchanges'.[118] To cling to entre-

117. *Scientific American*, 7 March 1900 (Supplement).
118. Werner Sombart, *Die deutsche Volkswirtschaft im 19. Jahrhundert und im Anfang des 20. Jahrhunderts* (Stuttgart, 1954; reprint of the 7th edn), p. 200.

The Apotheosis of Electricity.
Title page of the journal, *La Lumière électrique*, 1882

preneurial autonomy and energy independence in the new
world of the second Industrial Revolution would have been a
quixotic act. The new industries, electricity and chemicals, were
the breeding ground of the new faith in technical, scientific and
politico-economic planning that emerged after about 1900. The
engineers who increasingly replaced entrepreneurs in these

industries completed the transition from technical to economic reality. 'As this breed worked up into management and executive positions within the science-based corporations, they came to identify the advance of modern technology with the advance of these corporations.'[119] Around 1900 there was no contradiction in being an electrical engineer, a senior executive of an electrical concern and a convinced socialist. Charles Steinmetz, who combined all these positions — he was a manager at General Electric — believed that the large capitalist enterprise was 'the most efficient means of making individual development possible in our present state of civilization'.[120] (Lenin's famous formula: 'Electricity + Soviet power = Communism' is a radical echo of this social philosophy founded on electricity.)

What does all this have to do with the lamp?

Let us go back to the question of why psychological resistance to a central energy supply, so widespread in the nineteenth century, faded with the advent of the electric light bulb. We can now say that in addition to electricity's cleanliness, odourlessness and harmlessness, there was another factor that made it easier for people to accept a central energy source.

The nineteenth-century definition of a lamp *before* electrification was as individualistic as the mentality of enterprise capitalism. The new definition was as 'collective' as Steinmetz's opinion that the large enterprise guaranteed individual development. 'However perfect a lamp may be', wrote Parville in 1883, 'taken by itself it is not a complete lighting system. It is only one part of the whole system. One does not fill a lamp with electric current like oil.'[121]

An Imaginary Conversation

A few days ago, in one of the theatres with electric lighting, we chanced to overhear a conversation between an elegant lady and two well-spoken gentlemen in the row behind us.

119. David F. Noble, *America by Design: Science, Technology, and the Rise of Corporate Capitalism* (New York, 1977), p. 19.

120. *General Electric Review*, vol. 18 (1915), p. 810, quoted from ibid., p. 42.

121. de Parville, *L'Electricité*, p. 375.

Title page of the journal *La Lumière électrique*, 1886

'Look', said the lady, 'the gas flames are upside down.'
'You are mistaken, my dear', replied her husband, 'they are electric lamps!'
'Yes indeed', explained the third, 'they are Edison lamps.'
'That's nice', said the lady, 'but if one of those lamps were to break, would it still give out light?'
'I don't think so', replied her husband, 'because then it would no longer have any electricity.'

'Ah, then the electricity is in the chandelier?'

'Of course.'

'No', said the second gentleman, 'the electricity is in the cellar or behind the sets, and it gets into the lamps via the wiring.'

'But tell me', exclaimed the lady, 'if one were to break a wire, would the electricity leak out into the auditorium? Wouldn't that be dangerous for the audience?'

'My dear wife', said her husband, bringing the conversation to an end as the performance began, 'one can breathe electricity without the least danger. And in any case, it would rise and collect under the ceiling at once, so we would have nothing to fear.'[122]

122. 'L'Electricité', *Revue scientifique illustrée*, 1 January 1887.

The Street

Nightfall brings forces very different from those that rule the day. In the symbols and myths of most cultures, night is chaos, the realm of dreams, teeming with ghosts and demons as the oceans teem with fish and sea monsters. The night is feminine, just as the day is masculine, and like everything feminine, it holds both repose and terror. For the mythic imagination, night and the deluge are closely related. They are two sides of the chaos from which, according to Jewish, Egyptian and Babylonian creation myths, the world — light and dry land — came forth. Every time the sun rises, the world and the light are created anew; in every sunset the world and the light, the sphere of solidity and Apollonian masculinity, again descend into the flux of darkness.

The newer a culture is, the more it fears nightfall.

Each evening, the medieval community prepared itself for dark like a ship's crew preparing to face a gathering storm. At sunset, people began a retreat indoors, locking and bolting everything behind them. First the city gates, which had been opened at sunrise, were closed.[1] The same thing happened in individual houses. They were locked and often the city authorities took the keys for safekeeping overnight. A Paris decree of 1380, for example, prescribed: 'At night, all houses . . . are to be locked and the keys deposited with the magistrate. Nobody may then enter or leave a house unless he can give the magistrate a good reason for doing so'.[2] In big cities like Berlin and Vienna, similar regulations remained in force until well into the nineteenth century. Indeed, to the present day, a curious type of lock has survived in Berlin that forces the occupants to lock the front door of the house behind them.

We can push the analogy between night and the deluge, the urban population and a ship's crew, even further. While the inhabitants of a medieval town locked themselves into their

1. In Hamburg, perhaps Germany's most progressive city, the gates were still being locked at the end of the eighteenth century. Wolfgang Nahrstedt writes, 'Closing the gates severed the link with outside' (*Die Entstehung der Freizeit – Dargestellt am Beispiel Hamburgs*, Göttingen, 1972, p.88).

2. Quoted from A. Trébuchet, *Rechercher sur l'éclairage public de Paris* (Paris, 1843), p. 4.

houses like sailors battening down below decks, the night-watch patrolled outside, keeping a check on the noctural no-man's-land. Every night, a curfew (*Ausgangssperre, couvrefeu*) barred the people from the streets, something that nowadays only happens during times of civil unrest. Night-watchmen carried weapons and a torch with them on their rounds. Torches served to light the way, but their main function was to make their bearers, the forces of order, visible. The same applied to ordinary citizens if, by any chance, they had to venture out on to the streets by night. Anyone who did not carry a light was regarded as suspect and could immediately be arrested, like someone without papers. 'And no man walke after IX of the belle streken in the nyght withoute lyght or withoute cause reasonable in payne of empresonment', read an English decree of 1467.[3] Paris had a similar regulation, which stated that citizens had to carry a lantern after 9 p.m., 'or they run the risk of being arrested and imprisoned by the night patrol'.[4] As late as 1788, Johann Heinrich Jung stated in his *Lehrbuch der Staats-Polizey-Wissenschaft*: 'Anyone who is found at an unusual hour in an unusual place without a light must submit to the strictest investigation.'

The first attempts to install permanent public lighting were made in the sixteenth century. Authorities in the larger cities issued regulations to the effect that every house had to identify itself by displaying a light. In Paris, for example, Parliament decreed that 'during the months of November, December and January a lantern is to be hung out under the level of the first floor window sills before 6 o'clock every night. It is to be placed in such a prominent position that the street receives sufficient light.'[5] This was not yet street lighting, but simply an extension of the old duty to carry a torch after dark. This decree aimed less to illuminate the street than to make individual houses recognisable by forcing them to display 'navigation' lights, thus imposing structure and order on the city by night.

Out of these beginnings grew the first real, centrally organ-

---

3. Quoted from G.T. Salusbury-Jones, *Street Life in Medieval England* (Brighton, 1975), p. 139 (1st edn 1939).

4. Herlaut (Commandant), 'L'Eclairage des rues à Paris à la fin du 17e au 18e siècles', *Société de l'Histoire de Paris et de l'Ile-de-France. Mémoires*, Vol. 43, p. 133.

5. Quoted from ibid., p. 131.

Before the introduction of street lighting
(C. Lynken, *Aprilis*, about 1700. Archiv für Kunst und Geschichte.)

ised public lighting. In the late seventeenth century, lanterns were fixed on the streets, rather than on houses, at the initiative of the new absolutist state. Through this and other measures, it extended its order and control to the street. The police were the authority into whose jurisdiction these lanterns fell, for in those days they were not custodians of order in the modern sense, but had charge of the entire internal administration. As Albert Babeau put it: 'The sphere of police activity comprised the whole of the moral and material order. Their work consisted of prevention as well as suppression'.[6] The police of an absolutist state prescribed how bread should be baked, beer brewed and pigs slaughtered; they were concerned with every detail of daily life that could give rise to disorder and disturbances. Maintaining peace and order was their first duty. 'The attention of the police', wrote Johann Heinrich Gottlob von Justi in his *Grundsätze der Polizey-Wissenschaft* (1756)'must be primarily directed towards maintaining absolute peace in every town and city. As soon as a crowd gathers, they must be on the spot at once, investigate the cause and imprison the instigators, or remove the cause in some other way. At night, especially, when diligent, hard-working residents need peace, the police must try to prevent any commotion or uproar by means of strict measures and provisions.'[7] The street, the obvious scene of any possible disorder or uproar, naturally attracted the particular attention of the police. The streets of Paris, not yet patrolled and modernised by the police, seemed as dangerous as a jungle to the absolutist eye with its concern for order. Contemporary travel literature and the satirical verse of the period often bemoan the dangers of sinking in the mire of unpaved streets, breaking one's neck or being murdered at night. Boileau, for example, wrote in his sixth satire: 'Le bois le plus funeste et le moins frequenté/Est, au prix de Paris, un lieu de sûreté' (Compared with Paris, the darkest and loneliest forest is a safe retreat).

The police of the French absolutist state introduced a whole series of measures to deal with these conditions. The streets were cleaned and modernised in the widest sense, in a process that has been compared to Baron Haussmann's achievement 200 years later.[8] The first step was to remove the medieval shop signs, which projected far into the streets, obstructed the traffic

---

6. Albert Babeau, *La Ville sous l'Ancien Régime* (Paris, 1884; reprint New York, 1972), Vol. 1, p. 331.

7. Johann Heinrich Gottlob von Justi, *Grundsätze der Polizey-Wissenschaft* (Göttingen, 1756), pp. 264–5.

8. Leon Bernard, *The Emerging City: Paris in the Age of Louis XIV* (Durham, North Carolina, 1970), p. 283.

and blocked the long vistas so pleasing to the Baroque, absolutist mentality. As an English traveller, Martin Lister, noticed, the removal of these signs had a highly symbolic significance:

> Tis pretty to observe, how the King disciplines this great City, by small instances of Obedience. He caused them to take down all their signs at once, and not to advance them above a Foot or two from the Wall, nor to exceed such a small measure of square; which was readily done; so that the Signs obscure not the Streets at all, and make little or no Figure, as tho' there were none.[9]

Under absolutist rule, the foot as well as the eye fell on smooth, uniform planes, for laying pavements was another innovation of the period. Until about the middle of the seventeenth century, street paving and lighting were both more or less the private affair of residents, acting under instructions from the authorities. (Some of the household's responsibility for the street adjacent to it has survived to the present day in places where residents are obliged to keep the pavements free of snow in winter.) Well into the seventeenth century, matters such as the sort of lanterns to be hung out at night and the type of stones to be used in paving were left to the householder in the same way that equipping the soldiers in an army was left to the commanders of individual divisions. Gradually, however, the number of regulations multiplied, until in 1638 street paving became a public concern, centrally organised and financed by a new tax. It was carried out by a subcontractor appointed by the police. From now on, too, the police dictated exactly what paving stones were to look like, as in this directive dated 1729: 'The new paving stone is to be a cube, with sides measuring nine inches, and contractors may not reduce this size.'[10] The old paving stones bore the same relationship to the new ones as did the colourful, straggling armies of the Thirty Years' War to the regularly uniformed, standing armies of absolutism: in both cases, disorderly masses were transformed into neatly lined up, mathematically exact structures.

The same thing happened with street lighting when this was ✓

9. Martin Lister, *A Journey to Paris in the Year 1698* (London, 1699; reprint Chicago University Press, 1967), p. 17.

10. Quoted from Nicholas de la Mare, *Traité de la Police* (Paris, 1738), Vol. 4, p. 189.

Absolutism and public lighting.
A Louis XIV medallion, issued to commemorate the introduction of public
lighting in Paris, 1667.
(*Source*: d'Allemagne, *Histoire du luminaire*.)

introduced by royal decree in 1667, a decade and a half after the
defeat of the Fronde. What had begun as lighting on private
houses turned into 'a public service under the control of the
street police, carried out in line with the minute, arbitrary and
draconian police regulations of the day'.[11] The diversity of
private lanterns was replaced by a standard lantern, consisting
of a candle in a glass box. Initially, 2,700 such lanterns were
installed; in 1700 there were more than 5,000, and by the second
half of the eighteenth century the number had risen to about
8,000.[12]

Nothing shows the break with the older style of house lighting more clearly than the placement of the new lanterns. They
were attached to cables strung across the street so that they
hung exactly over the middle of the street, like small suns,
representing the Sun King, on whose orders they had been put

11. Herlaut, 'L'Eclairage des rues à Paris', p. 139.
12. These figures are taken from the following accounts: Eugène Defrance, *Histoire de
l'éclairage des rues de Paris* (Paris, 1904), gives the figure 2,736, without naming a source;
Herlaut, 'Eclairage des rues à Paris', who gives the figure of 5,470 lanterns for the year 1702,
and 6,408 for 1740 (p. 163), names contemporary police records as his source. In *Tableau de
Paris* (Amsterdam, 1782), Louis Sébastien Mercier speaks of 8,000 lanterns in the second half
of the eighteenth century, while Pierre Patte mentions only 6,777 (*De la manière la plus
avantageuse d'éclairer les rues d'une ville pendant la nuit*, Paris, 1766, p. 6).

up. This way of mounting the lanterns was remarked upon by foreign visitors and criticised by residents, who pointed to the fact that they obstructed the traffic.[13] At first glance it seems absurd that the same royal power that had freed the streets from the obstructive medieval shop signs should now hang up equally obstructive lanterns. But at second glance the logic becomes apparent: the lanterns showed who lit the streets and who ruled them. Paris was as much an exception in its peculiar method of hanging street lanterns as it was in the associated tradition of *lantern smashing*, which we will discuss later. Other absolutist regimes introduced police-administered street lighting in their cities towards the end of the seventeenth century. In these metropolises, the symbolism of domination was not quite so flagrant, though here too, *police lighting*, as it should, perhaps, be called, was also literally (i.e. physically) distant from the older style of lighting fixed to houses. In 1680, for example, the ruler of Prussia ordered Berlin's lanterns to be mounted on posts put up solely for this purpose (later to evolve into lamp posts), 'however much the residents oppose this on grounds of cost'.[14] A lantern that was no longer fixed to a house, but to a post in the middle of the street shone as 'publicly' as a lantern hanging over the middle of the street.

But there was also another, completely different method of public lighting. London, the commercial centre of the seventeenth and eighteenth centuries and in many respects the most modern city of the day, retained the old private form of house illumination into the eighteenth century. Not until 1736 was a certain uniformity imposed. Contractors in every district took over the lighting, which became a semi-public service, financed

13. There are several contradictory accounts of when this style of hanging lanterns came into use. According to a contemporary report such as Martin Lister's, lanterns were placed in this position from the start, hanging exactly over the middle of the street at intervals of about twenty paces and at a height of approximately 20 feet (*A Journey to Paris*, 1698, p. 25). Herlaut, however, normally a meticulous historian of Paris street lighting, claimed that initially lanterns 'were not hung over the middle of the street but attached to house walls by means of gallows-shaped fixtures' ('L'Eclairage des rues à Paris', p. 157). He reported that lanterns were not hung over the middle of the street until the 1760s, when a new type of lantern, the *réverbère*, was introduced. One reason for this inconsistency may have been that the lanterns mounted on fixtures might have belonged to an earlier period of house illumination. Apart from these, of course, lanterns *were* mounted in this way in large squares (and possibly very wide streets) that could not be spanned by a rope.

14. *Krünitz' Ökonomisch-technologische Encyclopädie* (Berlin, 1794), Vol. 65, p. 408.

from the taxes of individual householders. Until well into the eighteenth century, both the organisation and the brightness of London's street lighting compared unfavourably with those of Paris, as this contemporary description by William Maitland shows: 'Till this time, the Streets of London were perhaps worse illuminated by Night than those of any other great City, which was entirely owing to bad Management.'[15] The archaic state of London's lighting reflected the no less antiquated state of its police. Until Robert Peel's reforms at the beginning of the nineteenth century, the London police were organised more or less as they had been since the Middle Ages — less as a police force than as a collection of local keepers of the peace. They were mostly 'sleepy-headed old watchmen', who could not be compared with the feared police patrols of Paris. In London, the watchmen's duties were 'crying the hour after the chimes, taking precautions for the prevention of fire, proclaiming tidings of foul or fair weather, and awakening at daybreak all those who intended to set out on a journey'.[16] To the present day, the London police differ from those of all other European metropolises in that they do not carry guns.

Something else must have been done to keep order in London's dim and unpoliced streets, for such a highly developed city could not have gone without protection at night. It seems that in England — and later in the United States as well — security depended less on police surveillance, discipline and deterrence than on mechanical means such as locks and bolts. The fact that the English-speaking world possessed many highly developed mechanisms for locking things up, from the Yale lock to the safe (we could even call it a lock-up culture) supports this thesis. Mechanical locks secure a private space that, regardless of its surroundings, is designed primarily to protect property against appropriation by others. Police surveillance, by contrast, secures public spaces, its only purpose is to maintain law and order in public. We can assume that in the seventeenth and eighteenth centuries there was a direct link between public lighting and private locks. In Paris, with its modern lighting and policing, doors were probably locked and bolted less securely

15. William Maitland, *The History and Survey of London* (London, 1760), Vol. 1, p. 565.

16. William C. Sidney, *England and the English in the 18th Century* (London, 1892), Vol. 1, p. 17.

than in London, where locks on the doors had to compensate
for the security that the weak police and public lighting could
not provide.

The very different roles of public torch bearers in London and
Paris again shows how much more closely public lighting was
tied to policing in the French city. Like other European cities,
London and Paris had possessed 'mobile' public lighting in the
form of linkmen since the seventeenth century. Pedestrians
could hire them like cabs to light the way home. In Paris, torch
bearers were often police spies or informers. In his *Tableau de
Paris*, Mercier wrote:

> The nocturnal wanderers with their torches are in the service of the
> police and see everything that happens; thieves who want to force
> open locks in the back streets can never be sure that their unexpected
> lights will not turn up. . . . The torch-bearer goes to bed very late
> and next day reports everything he noticed to the police. Nothing is
> more effective in maintaining order and preventing various mishaps
> than these torches, which are carried around here and there; their
> sudden appearance forestalls many a nocturnal crime. At the slight-
> est disturbance the torch-bearers run to the watch-house and give
> evidence about what happened.[17]

It was well known that London's linkmen, by contrast, had
close contacts with, or even belonged to, the criminal under-
world: 'Far more often than not these "servants of the public"
were hand in glove with footpads and highwaymen, and would
rarely think twice on receiving a signal from such accomplices of
extinguishing the link and slipping away.'[18] In his description of
London customs, *Trivia*, John Gay, author of *The Beggar's Opera*,
warns the nocturnal passerby:

> Though thou art tempted by the Linkman's call
> Yet trust him not along the lonely wall,
> In the midway he'll quench the flaming brand,
> And share the booty with the pilf'ring band.[19]

---

17. Louis-Sébastian Mercier, *Paris am Vorabend der Revolution* (Karlsruhe, 1967), pp. 67–8.
(This is a selection from *Tableau de Paris*.)
18. Sidney, *England and the English*, p. 15.
19. Quoted from ibid., p. 16.

How bright did the new lanterns really make the street? Was it true that, as many occasional poems claimed enthusiastically in Paris in 1667, night had been turned into day?

> Il fera comme en plein midi,
> Clair la nuit dedans chaque rue,
> De longue ou de courte étendue,
> Par le grand nombre de clartés
> Qu'il fait mettre de tous costés
> En autant de belles lanterns![20]

Street lights that burn steadily all through the night and all year long are not yet a hundred years old. From the end of the seventeenth to the end of the nineteenth century, public lighting was still completely tied to the rhythms of nature. During the summer months it was restricted to a few hours or not used at all, as in the early days of public lighting in Paris when it was put on only between the end of October and the beginning of April.[21] When the moon shone, too, they did without street lighting. 'When the grand light that rules the night lights up the street sufficiently, lanterns are superfluous', writes Krünitz in his Encyclopedia. He continues: 'As moonlight is sometimes bright and sometimes weak, and as the moon sometimes rises early and sometimes late, these changes must be taken into account. Throughout the year the times when the lanterns are to be used must be specified, as well as the precise times at which they are to be lit and extinguished'.[22] This was done with the aid of lighting schedules, which calculated the exact times of sunrise and sunset as well as the hours of moonlight for each month. On the basis of this data, the police issued detailed lighting instructions, such as the following example from 1719, in which a Paris district commissar also specified the size of candles to be used on various days:

On 1 December a half candle (1/8 pound) is to be lit. From 2 to 21

---

20. (The night will be lit up as bright as day, in every street, be it short or long, by the many lights that shine forth from the beautiful and equally numerous lamps.) Anonymous, *Gazette de Robinet*, 29 October 1667 (quoted from Defrance, *Histoire de l'éclairage*, p. 37).

21. Herlaut, 'L'Eclairage des rues à Paris', p. 163.

22. *Krünitz' Ökonomisch-technologische Encyclopädie*, pp. 353–4.

December inclusive, whole candles (1/4 pound) are to be used. On 22 and 23 December no candles are to be lit. On 24 December, Christmas Eve, twelve-pound candles are to be burned. From 25 to 27 December, no lighting is to be used at all. On 28, 29 and 30 December half candles are to be lit, and on 31 December, a whole candle.[23]

Dependence on natural rhythms did not change with the introduction of gas lighting. In about 1860 in Leipzig, 'lighting was used, taking into account moonlit nights on which street lighting is normally reduced to a small number of flames'.[24] In Paris, two types of street lanterns had developed by the 1840s, 'permanent lanterns which burn from sunset to sunrise, and variable lanterns, which are lit only when the moonlight is not bright enough to light the streets.'[25] Early in the twentieth century, public lighting in many cities was still regulated according to moonlight schedules. On clear moonlit nights lanterns were turned off earlier than usual, mostly shortly after midnight.[26]

It was slowly, almost reluctantly, that street lighting became independent of natural light conditions. But there was a gradual tendency to create illuminated areas that existed in their own right, unconnected to the glow of moon and stars. The first step in this direction was to decrease the space between lanterns. There is no reliable data on this, but we can assume that the lanterns installed in Paris in 1667 were not closely spaced. Two lanterns were put in short streets, one at each end; in longer streets an additional lantern was placed in the middle.[27] In time, the variable distance between lanterns was standardised and reduced to about twenty metres.[28] While the low illuminating power of the lanterns meant that they did not cast an even pool of light, they did form something like a connected chain of light.

Another step towards making the light on streets brighter and more concentrated was to strengthen the light source itself using optical aids such as lenses and reflectors. As early as the end of the seventeenth century, lanterns with specially cut glass

23. Quoted from Herlaut, 'L'Eclairage des rues à Paris', p. 167.
24. C.F.A. Jahn, *Die Gasbeleuchtung* (Leipzig, 1862), p. 95.
25. A. Trébuchet, *Recherches sur l'éclairage public de Paris*, p. 57.
26. *Lectures on Illuminating Engineering* (Baltimore, 1911), Vol. 2, p. 824.
27. Defrance, *Histoire de l'éclairage*, p. 37.
28. Herlaut, 'L'Eclairage des rues à Paris', p. 157.

Reflector lamp (*réverbère*), Paris, mid-eighteenth century.
(*Source*: d'Allemagne, *Histoire du luminaire*.)

Detail of a *réverbère*.
Left: the oil reservoir with the wick. *Right*: the
concave reflector.
(*Source*: d'Allemagne, *Histoire du luminaire*.)

that focused the glow like a flood light had been used in Paris. This innovation failed, perhaps because of the lack of a central organisation for public lighting. But in 1760 Paris witnessed the development of a new type of lantern that was to go down in the history not only of street lighting and the police but also that of the French Revolution. The reflector lantern, or *réverbère* — its original French name, which we will use here — was designed for a competition held by the Académie des Sciences in 1763 at the suggestion of the Paris police chief de Sartine, who donated the prize of 2,000 francs. The prize was to be given 'sur la meilleure manière d'éclairer pendant la nuit les rues d'une grande ville en combinant ensemble la clarté, la facilité du service et l'économie'. Lavoisier, just twenty years old at the time, sent in an entry which did not win the official prize, but earned him a medal as a personal mark of honour from the king. The type of lantern Lavoisier proposed closely resembled the prototype that was eventually constructed.

Two technical improvements made the *réverbère* shine many times more brightly than the lanterns in use up to that time. It used an oil lantern with several wicks, not just one, instead of a candle, and the light thus gained was further intensified by means of two reflectors. A hemispherical reflector attached above the flame collected the light that had dissipated unused in the old lanterns, and cast it down on to the street; a slightly concave reflector next to the flame directed its light sideways.

Like the first lanterns one hundred years before, *réverbères* were enthusiastically hailed as artificial suns that turned night into day. A report prepared for the police chief de Sartine suggests that 'the amount of light they cast makes it difficult to imagine that anything brighter could exist'.[29] Mercier, who thought that the old lamps 'cast only a weak, flickering and uncertain light, which was, moreover, impaired by dangerous shadows', was full of praise for the new ones: 'Now the city is extremely brightly lit. The combined force of 1,200 *réverbères* creates an even, lively and lasting light.'[30] Statements such as

---

29. 'Mémoire sur l'administration de la Police en France contenant les éclaircissements demandés à ce sujet par Monsier l'Ambassadeur de Vienne. . . etc.', first published as 'La Police de Paris en 1770', in *Mémoires de la Société de l'Histoire de Paris et de l'Ile-de-France*. Vol. 5, pp. 1 – 131. Quoted from Herlaut, 'L'Eclairage des rues à Paris', pp. 252.

30. Mercier, *Tableau de Paris*, Vol. 1, p. 212.

Night scene with *réverbère*.
(*Source: Les Nuits de Paris*, Paris, 1788.)

these say little more about the real increase in brightness than
do occasional poems, which at this time, too, celebrated the
'globes brillantes' and 'astres nouveaux'. Mercier provides a nice
example of how quickly a new level of light lost its glamour as
soon as it became normal. In the first volume of his *Tableau de
Paris*, Mercier praises *réverbères* in the words just quoted; a little

later, by volume ten, he already finds them inadequate. 'These lights cast nothing but darkness made visible. . . . From a distance they hurt the eyes, from close up they give hardly any light, and standing directly underneath one, one might as well be in the dark.'[31] Although it is impossible to reconstruct exactly how bright the *réverbères* really were, we can assume that the stronger, more focused and directed light they cast made it possible to illuminate a section of the street effectively for the first time. This was definite progress over the old lanterns, which had in fact never been more than orientation lights or position markers.

Surprisingly enough, the new light capacity available was not fully exploited. The old lanterns were not replaced one for one by *réverbères*; instead, the total number of lanterns was reduced by almost the exact proportion by which *réverbères* outshone the old lanterns. The 6,000 to 8,000 old lanterns[32] in Paris were replaced by 1,200 *réverbères* and the distance between them was increased from 20 to 60 metres.[33] In other words, the light intensity gained by technical improvements was lost again by spreading the lanterns more thinly on the ground. However brightly *réverbères* shone, they could not cast enough light to illuminate a gap of 60 metres. Their effect was, in fact, no different from that of the old lanterns — they functioned as position markers or beacons. Although they cast a considerably larger circle of light, it remained isolated — *réverbères* stood out like islands of light in the darkness.

It is something of a mystery how the eighteenth-century eye saw night-time Paris, with its scattered patches of light, as a brightly lit city. Perhaps two different levels of perception overlapped here, so that *symbolic* light was seen as *actual* light. The brightness of the lantern itself, which had undoubtedly increased, could have been perceived as the brightness of the street, although this had in fact hardly changed. The history of the development of public lighting suggests that this was indeed the case. From the start, the lights that people were obliged to carry with them at night served primarily as signs of identification. The fact that torches also lit up the path for whoever was

---

31. Ibid., Vol. 10, p. 147; quoted from Herlaut, 'L'Eclairage des rues à Paris', p. 260.
32. See note 12.
33. Herlaut, 'L'Eclairage des rues à Paris', p. 252.

carrying them had no significance for public order. When the authorities installed the first public lanterns in the seventeenth century, it was quite obvious that the lantern itself was more important than its function of lighting the street. The streets must have been dimly lit, despite all contemporary protestations to the contrary, since linkmen remained part of the nocturnal street scene until the early nineteenth century.[34] Not until the late nineteenth century, when industrial production made it possible to flood the streets with light, did public lighting become street lighting in the modern sense. But if public lighting in the seventeenth and eighteenth centuries did not really light up the street, then what was the point of it?

Gaston Bachelard, the author of a psychoanalytical-poetic interpretation of fire and of candlelight, has developed a psychology of lantern light that clarifies the origins and nature of public lighting. 'Everything that casts a light sees' ('Tout ce qui brille voit') — this is Bachelard's psychological and mythological starting point.[35] He goes on to describe the process of surveillance, counter-surveillance and mutual surveillance that is set in motion when a lantern is lit.[36] Anyone who is in the dark and sees a light in the distance feels that he or she is being observed, because 'this lantern in the distance is not "sufficient unto itself". It constantly strives outwards. It watches so unflaggingly that it watches *over* things.'[37] Someone who feels observed in this way tries to turn the tables. He extinguishes his own lantern so that he is not exposed defenceless to the gaze of the other, whom he can now observe without himself being observed. 'The lonely dreamer who sees himself being watched begins to watch his watcher. He hides his own lantern in order to expose the lantern of the other.' The 'psychologie des hostilités intimes'

34. 'The street lighting was so inadequate that when going out at night, one was generally obliged to make use of the services of the linkmen standing on every street corner' (*Souvenirs et Causeries*, 1781, quoted from Defrance, *Histoire de l'éclairage*, p. 76). 'Nothing was more annoying for the foreign visitor far from his lodgings at night. . . than not being able to find one of the helpful guides with their numbered torches' (F.-M. Marchant, *Le nouveau Conducteur de l'Ètranger à Paris en 1820*, Paris, 1820, p. 14).

35. Gaston Bachelard, *Die Poetik des Raumes* (Munich, 1967), p. 48; Waldemar Deonna, *Le symbolisme de l'oeil* (Berne, 1965), pp. 251ff.

36. The fact that Bachelard's discussion of this is based on a fictional situation in the novel *Hyacinthe*, by Henri Bosco, need not concern us here as the context has no significance for us.

37. Gaston Bachelard, *La flamme d'une chandelle* (Paris, 1961), p. 102 (original emphasis).

(Bachelard) that develops between two people who both possess light arises out of its dual function as an instrument of surveillance and a mark of identification that exposes one to the surveillance of others. This double significance lies behind the medieval regulations requiring anyone who went out at night to identify himself by carrying a light. Any process of identification that was not reciprocal would have destroyed the 'balance of power' of light carriers, rather like unilateral disarmament in an armed society. The takeover by the state of individual identification by light, institutionalised in the form of public lighting in the seventeenth century, can in fact be compared to the roughly contemporaneous development of a state weapons monopoly in the army and the police. The unstable balance, the 'psychologie des hostilités intimes', between private individuals was replaced by a state monopoly on light and weapons. People submitted to it because it promised to guarantee stability and security. But although public lighting was welcomed as holding out the promise of security, it was also a police institution and, as such, attracted all the hostility traditionally directed at the police.

Lantern Smashing

'After midnight, every street light is worth a host of watchmen' (E. Kolloff, *Paris, Reisehandbuch*, 1849). This was one of the principles of maintaining law and order in late-eighteenth-century, pre-revolutionary Paris. By day, 1,500 uniformed police were on the streets.[38] By night, 3,500 lanterns (*réverbères*)[39] achieved the same result.

The police budget shows how important public lighting was in the security apparatus. Lighting accounted for 15 per cent of the total, making it the largest single item in the police budget apart from the watch (Le Guet).[40] Mercier, who defines the police apparatus as a *machine* for maintaining order in Paris, lists its most important components as 'the street lights and *réverbères*,

---

38. Alan John Williams, *The Police of Paris 1718–1789* (University Microfilms, Ann Arbor, 1975), p. 358.

39. Herlaut, 'L'Éclairage des rues à Paris', p. 258; the exact number is 3,528.

40. Williams, *The Police of Paris*, p. 362.

the various guard units . . . and the torch bearers'.[41] In this picture of order and security, illumination meshes seamlessly with the whole range of police methods; indeed, lanterns almost seem to dominate everything else.

It comes as no surprise, therefore, that from the start the street lanterns of Paris provoked aggression from below. 'Drunkards and debauchees, wandering through the streets at night, amused themselves by smashing them with their sticks, if they could reach high enough.'[42] When the *réverbères* were hung so high that they were out of reach of sticks,[43] a new method of destroying them became popular. It consisted of cutting the ropes on which the lanterns hung, letting them smash on the pavement.

Whatever the details and methods, smashing lanterns was obviously an extremely enjoyable activity. Here, there is only room for a brief sketch of its psychological significance. Its main appeal was putting out the light. The act of extinguishing a fire (the psychoanalytical archetype is urinating on the fire) confers a feeling of omnipotence. Destroying lanterns in the seventeenth and eighteenth centuries offered the additional satisfaction of symbolically unseating the authority they represented: the darkness that prevailed after the lanterns had gone out stood for disorder and freedom. Added to this visual experience of omnipotence was a no less pleasurable aural one. The sound of breaking glass is like an explosion. Something that a moment ago was solid, an object with a highly symbolic significance, is suddenly wiped out. The desire to wreak such destruction and also to experience a symbolic sexual release in the loud splintering of breaking glass were probably the deeper motives behind lantern smashing.

Every attack on a street lantern was a small act of rebellion against the order that it embodied and was punished as such. In Paris, destroying lanterns was not treated as disorderly conduct (*contravention aux ordonnances*) but as a criminal offence not far short of lese-majesty.[44] 'If any Man break them', an English

41. Mercier, *Tableau de Paris*, Vol. 1, p. 199.

42. Herlaut, 'L'Eclairage des rues à Paris', p. 226.

43. 'Since *réverbères* have been introduced, the fact that they are hung so high protects them from brutal attack by nocturnal revellers' (Retif de la Bretonne, *Les Nuits des Paris: Oeuvres*, Paris, 1930, p. 68).

44. Herlaut, 'L'Eclairage des rues à Paris', p. 226.

Lanterns and *lanterner*. In July 1789 two of the most hated representatives of the *ancien régime*, Foulon and Berthier, were hanged using the fixture of a lantern attached to the Hôtel de Ville in Paris. (The lantern itself is lying on the pavement.) Subsequently, their severed heads were put on public display. This particular lantern was especially symbolic because it was in the immediate vicinity of a bust of Louis XIV.
(*Source*: d'Allemagne, *Histoire du luminaire*.)

travel writer reports in the late seventeenth century, 'he is forthwith sent to the Gallies; and there were three young Gentlemen of good families, who were in Prison for having done it in a Frolick, and could not be released thence in some Months; and that not without the deligent Application of good Friends at Court.'[45] In London, where street lanterns did not symbolise an absolute monarchy, punishments for the same crime, or rather offence, were correspondingly milder: a fine of twenty shillings for the first offence, forty shillings in case of recurrence, and three pounds for a third offence.[46]

During the Paris revolutions and rebellions of the nineteenth century, lantern smashing — until then an individual, libertine

---

45. Lister, *A Journey to Paris*, p. 25.
46. Maitland, *The History and Survey of London*, p. 566.

phenomenon — became a collective, plebeian movement. But before it reached this stage, there was an unforeseen and lethal interlude. In the summer of 1789, the meaning of the French verb *lanterner* changed. Mercier describes this change as follows: 'Originally, this word meant "to do nothing" or "to waste one's time". At the beginning of the Revolution, it meant "to hang a man from a lantern".'[47] This is how popular revenge vented itself in the first weeks of the Revolution, before the Committee of Public Safety and the guillotine imposed their order on revolutionary justice. The first victims were two of the most hated representatives of the *ancien régime*, Foulon and Berthier, who, on 22 July 1789, were strung up on a lantern fixed to the front of the Hôtel de Ville. Unlike most lanterns, which hung from ropes stretched across the street, this one was attached to the wall by means of a gallows-shaped fixture. This unusual feature can be explained by the fact that the lantern was not in a street but on a square, the Place de Grève (the traditional execution site), which could not be spanned by a rope.[48]

The most obvious reason for using this particular fixture for an execution was that it was shaped like a gallows. But something else must have been at work too, as the streets of Paris were full of objects just as well suited to the purpose — there were many trees, for example, and sign-boards of shops and inns were still sufficiently numerous and quite strong enough. This was more likely a case of settling accounts in a manner both

---

47. Quoted from Herlaut (Le Commandant), *L'Éclairage de Paris à l'époque révolutionnaire* (Paris, 1933), p. 18.

48. See p. 87, n. 13. A German report of 1791, explaining how victims were hanged on 'ordinary' lantern fixtures, is frequently quoted in the literature, with slight variations: 'In the early days of the Revolution in Paris, the *réverbères*, or street lanterns, became something very terrible indeed because of the executions in which they were involved. In Germany people seem to think that hangings took place on lampposts, but this is not correct: the ropes on which the lanterns are suspended over the middle of the street were used. These ropes are generally attached to houses and are lowered with the lanterns on one side of the street over a kind of pulley arrangement when the lanterns need to be filled with oil or lit. The end of the rope is wound around a hook. After this operation, it is locked up in a niche in the wall behind a small, iron door. These little doors were forced open and the lantern lowered and taken off the rope. In its stead, an offender would be hoisted into the air. But these ropes were designed to carry the weight of a lantern, not of a person, and so they often broke. Not infrequently, the hapless offender had to be taken to four or even six *réverbères* before a rope strong enough to survive this treatment was found' (Schulz, *Paris und die Pariser*, Berlin, 1791, quoted from Krünitz' *Ökonomischtechnologische Encyclopädie*, Vol. 65, p. 397).

Lanterns in the Revolution: contemporary caricatures
An English caricature (*above*) French caricatures (pp. 102–3)

Eh, l'abbé l'abbé, prend garde à la Lanterne.
Car ils sont plus fins que nous.

Le Général d'Alton poursuivi par les Reverberes Patriotiques.

Pet... Mer deux

Va... puisque tu ne veux pas nous donner
pour boire, Nous allons filer la Corde
paroles de Ces Dames Ce 19 7.bre 1791

real and symbolic. Hauling down the lantern and replacing it
with a representative of the old order bloodily reversed the
ancient symbolism. If lanterns represented the *ancien régime*,
then a hanged Foulon and a hanged Berthier represented the
unleashed power of the people. There may have been a further
symbolic reason for using that specific lantern on the Hôtel de
Ville: a bust of Louis XIV was mounted in a niche above it.
There, popular justice could take place right under the eyes of
the king.

This by no means complete account of the prelude to lantern
smashing shows that lanterns were not chosen accidentally.[49]

49. Another reason for the unpopularity of public lighting was that the residents of a
street were obliged to light the lanterns and keep them burning the whole night through.
This last survival from the period of private-house illumination was not abolished until
1759, when professional lamplighters were employed. Citizens did not regard this as an
echo of the old freedoms; rather, they saw it as a constant reminder of the arbitrariness of
the police. If a lantern went out in the middle of the night, the watch did not remedy the
situation, but got the person responsible for the lanterns out of bed so that he could replace
the light (Herlaut, *'L'Eclairage de Paris à l'époque révolutionnaire*, p. 185). The person responsi-

Rather, long-pent-up grievances vented themselves in this choice. The literature and folklore of the period, which immediately took up the theme, show us the extent to which the Revolutionary masses of 1789 were obsessed with the image of the lantern. Camille Desmoulins called his famous speech in the summer of 1789 'Discours de la lanterne aux Parisiens', and he was nicknamed 'Procureur de la lanterne'. And the chorus of the revolutionary song 'Ça ira', which preceded *La Marseillaise* in the same way that the lantern foreshadowed the guillotine, goes, 'Les aristocrates à la lanterne!' (After concluding the present study, I discovered Klaus Herding's essay 'Diogenes als Held' in *Boreas, Münstersche Beiträge zur Archäeologie*, vol. 5, 1982, pp. 232–54. In it, the lantern motif in the caricature and journalism of the Enlightenment and the revolutionary period is traced back to the Diogenes topos. Without being aware of each other, the iconography of the lantern and its real history proceeded hand in hand.)

Hanging people from lanterns played no further part in the Paris revolutions and rebellions of the nineteenth century. This activity was replaced by lantern smashing, which at first glance looks like a revival of the seventeenth- and eighteenth-century tradition. According to the forces of the state, attacks on lanterns were nothing short of wanton vandalism by nocturnal rowdies. Maxime Du Camp describes such attacks from the perspective of the Second Empire:

> During the rebellions, of which there were many in the Restoration period and under Louis Philippe, street lanterns were like a red rag

---

ble for the lanterns in one or more streets (*commis allumeur*), however, was not simply appointed by the police but was elected every year by a meeting of residents. The aversion to this obligation took on quite class-specific, even rebellious forms in these elections. Petty bourgeois residents voted 'par manière de protestation, soit de hauts personnages, soit de riches bourgeois' (ibid, p. 208). To be sure, if the person elected in this way protested, the police superintendent responsible would as a rule declare the election null and void, and appoint one of the petty bourgeois residents as *commis allumeur*.

Another contemporary motif was the petty bourgeois view of the night as the time and place of (aristocratic) pleasures totally foreign to the bourgeoisie, which they had no reason to encourage by providing street lighting. We read in a pamphlet of 1749: 'If there is anyone without the slightest interest in this duty, then it is the artisan. Exhausted from the efforts of the day, he is incapable of participating in the pleasures of the night' (quoted from ibid., p. 211). This may also explain why the tax that financed public lighting, the 'taxe des boues et lanternes', 'was one of the most unpopular ones' (ibid., pp. 139–40).

to a bull for all those good-for-nothings who are glorified in literature these days. Whenever a crowd gathered, that lot — all they deserved was the whip — would appear and swarm around like bees around a honeypot. They would throw stones at lanterns, breaking the glass. The worst of them would climb onto the shoulders of their comrades and cut the ropes on which the lanterns hung. Then they would make off as quickly as they could, before the police patrol, alerted by the noise of the lantern smashing on the pavement, could get there. Sometimes they would reduce a whole street to complete darkness in no more than fifteen minutes.[50]

Lantern smashing appeared as an adjunct to general revolt for the first time in July 1830. Contemporary reports give a different impression of it from Du Camp. A German eye-witness, for example, described it as follows: 'The populace, furious, runs through the streets, smashing lanterns, challenging the bourgeoisie to fight, and swearing that it will have vengeance.'[51] Or to quote a French report: 'In the midst of these horrors [the street fighting of 27 July, the first day of the July Revolution] night fell over the city, and now the populace began smashing the *revérbères*. . . . Along with the *revérbères*, all other symbols of the treacherous king's authority were destroyed — they did not want anything to remind them of him.'[52] This was no longer a case of a few mischievous nocturnal revellers destroying a lantern or two; now the 'populace' was involved, and its aim was to extinguish *all* lanterns. The fact that lanterns are mentioned in the same breath as the other hated emblems of domination shows that the old symbolism was still very much alive. We even find a new variant on the reversal of the lantern's symbolic significance — a further development on the 1789 practice of hanging people from the ropes holding up lanterns. Here it is, as observed by a German visitor: 'The populace vented its anger on all the signs of royal power: escutcheons, at first draped with black crape, were taken down or smashed and hung on lantern cords.'[53]

50. Maxime Du Camp, *Paris: Ses origines, ses fonctions et sa vie* (Paris, 1875), Vol. 5, p. 285.

51. *Briefe aus Paris, geschrieben während der großen Volkswoche im Juli 1830, von einem deutschen Augenzeugen* (Hamburg, 1831), p. 47.

52. *Les barricades immortelles du peuple de Paris. Relation historique, militaire et anecdotique des jours à jamais mémorables des 26, 27, 28 et 29 juillet 1830. Par P. Cuisin* (Paris, 1830), pp. 129–30.

53. Johann Heinrich Schnitzler, *Ausführlicher Bericht eines Augenzeugen über die letzten*

But it was not just that the rebels had a gift for symbolic gesture. Lantern smashing was above all a practical strategy in street fighting against the forces of the state. The darkness that spread as lanterns were smashed created an area in which government forces could not operate. The eye-witness we have just quoted wrote: 'As lanterns were smashed and darkness descended, the streets were too unsafe for royal troops to be allowed to stay there. They retreated, behind their cannons and with constant skirmishes, to Louis XIV Square. From there, they dared to send out patrols, but only to the main roads and *quais*.'[54]

Lantern smashing erected a wall of darkness, so to speak, protecting an area from incursion by government forces. It went hand in hand with another technique of nineteenth-century street fighting: the erection of real walls, or barricades. The barricade acted as a physical impediment matching the visual one provided by the unilluminated night. 'Streets where attacks were expected, or that the rebels wanted to hold, were blocked with wooden implements, planks and stones, the lanterns were removed or smashed, and weapons were collected and cartridges prepared.'[55] The result of this double barricading has been described as follows: 'Stripped of all its lanterns and completely barricaded, Paris was made impregnable within a few hours.'[56] With the simultaneous appearance of barricades and smashed lanterns in July 1830, the repressed returned in a classical way. These revolutionary acts reversed the order that absolutism had imposed on the street 150 years earlier. Tearing up the paving stones and re-assembling them as barricades freed the earth to return to its 'natural' state, which had disappeared in the seventeenth century; extinguishing the artificial light of the lanterns restored the natural darkness of the night. The soil below the pavements, and the clear, dark night sky above the smashed lanterns — so goes, more or less, a poetic description, reissued in May 1968, of nature and society liberated by revolution.

Auftritte der französischen Revolution während der zwei Wochen vom 26. Julius bis zum 9. August 1830 (Stuttgart and Tübingen, 1830), p. 37.

54. Ibid., p. 36.
55. Ibid., p. 37.
56. *Les barricades immortelles* . . ., p. 150.

In the wake of the July Revolution, the paving stones of Paris became a powerful literary motif. Pierre Citron writes: 'After the three days, paving stones are ubiquitous.'[57] He points out that the word *pavé* occurs forty-three times in poems written between 1830 and 1833 — in the poetry written between August and December 1830 alone, it appears eighteen times.[58] Most praised of all was the transformation of pavements into barricades. Victor Hugo noted in his diary: 'The pavement is the most splendid symbol of the people. One tramples on it until it dashes one's head to pieces'.[59] He is also the author of the line 'Under the living pavement, that rumblingly assembles'.[60] Adolphe Dumas wrote:

> Les Pavés! les Pavés!
> D'eux-mêmes, en remparts, comme soldats, levés
> Arrêtent les assauts. . .[61]

Apolitical poets as well as revolutionary ones wrote of the pavements. Here the pavement appears as the street's armour, intact, not yet broken open by revolution, a symbol of 'ugliness, hardness, colourlessness — in short, unnaturalness'.[62] This poetry shows pavements and street lighting as historically interlocked. The reflection of lantern light on the pavement became a poetic motif for loneliness, sorrow and coldness.

> Pour soleil des lanternes
> Qui de leurs reflets ternes
> Baignent les pavés gris
> (Gautier)[63]

> Sur le pavé noirci les blafardes lanternes

57. Pierre Citron, *La Poésie de Paris dans la littérature française de Rousseau à Baudelaire*, 2 vols. (Paris, 1961), Vol. 1, p. 233.

58. Ibid.

59. Quoted from ibid., Vol. 1, p. 433 (*Journal 1830–1848*).

60. Quoted from ibid., Vol. 1, p. 233 ('A la Colonne').

61. (The paving stones! the paving stones! Piled up in bulwarks, like soldiers, they halt attacks.) Quoted from ibid., Vol. 1, p. 233 ('Les Trois Journées').

62. Ibid., Vol. 1, p. 435.

63. (Lanterns as suns, that flood the grey pavements with their lustreless light.) Quoted from ibid., Vol. 1, p. 434.

Versaient un jour douteux plus triste que la nuit
(Musset)[64]

La lumière glacée aux vitres des lanternes
Miroitait tristement sur le pavé boueux
(Esquiros).[65]

Pierre Citron, who has collected these examples, comments: 'The lights of Paris, so often a symbol of brightness and cheerfulness, seem to be darkened and soiled, as it were, by contact with the pavement.'[66]

Poetic treatments of lantern light reflected in the waters of the Seine confirm Citron's view. Alphonse Esquiros, for whom lantern light and pavements evoke sadness, sees the light playing over the Seine quite differently: 'I love the reflection of the *revérbères* on the waves.'[67] Similarly, Musset writes:

Que j'aimais ce temps gris, ces passants, et la Seine
Sous ses mille falots assise en souveraine.[68]

The river, symbol of the restless life, is the opposite of the pavement — a piece of freely flowing nature in the middle of the city that can reflect even artificial light naturally.

But let us go back to the smashing of lanterns. What sort of darkness spread when lanterns were broken?

Descriptions read like illustrations of what Mercier had predicted fifty years earlier when he wrote, referring to the police *machine* (that could not have been a machine without lighting), 'if it were ever brought to a halt, then Paris would be exposed to all the terrors of a captured city'.[69] To the contemporary observer, the city stripped of light and the military seemed like a medieval city after dark: 'It is difficult to imagine the total

---

64. (On to the blackish pavement the leaden lanterns cast their uncertain light that was more melancholy than the night.) Quoted from ibid., Vol. 1, p. 435.

65. (The cold light of the lanterns was reflected sadly in the dirty pavement.) Quoted from ibid.

66. Quoted from ibid.

67. Quoted from ibid., Vol. 2, p. 177.

68. (How much I loved this grey hour, the strollers and the Seine, lit up by its thousand majestic torches.) Quoted from ibid., Vol. 1, p. 212.

69. *Tableau de Paris*, p. 199. The passage quoted here immediately follows the passage quoted on p. 98 above (n. 41).

darkness into which this big city was plunged when its lighting was destroyed. Locked doors of shops and houses, and lowered blinds in the windows conveyed the impression of a deserted city, visited by the plague. A terrible silence completed the picture of horror and threat.'[70] State power, impotent in the darkness created by the rebels, reacted by repeating a call it had already issued in the sixteenth century. Once again, citizens were urged to identify themselves by displaying lights, thus bringing the situation under control. 'Inhabitants of Paris', goes an appeal made by the Chief of the Paris police in July 1830, 'keep your distance to these wretches; do not let an imprudent curiosity mislead you into taking part in these riots. Stay inside your houses; put lights in your windows at night to illuminate the street; prove, by your prudence and your sober behaviour, that you have nothing to do with scenes that would put you to shame.'[71]

In Victor Hugo's novel *Les Misérables*, the play, or rather the struggle between light and darkness during a rebellion, unfolds in two scenes that seem like a distillation of history. Let's start with the scene in which Gavroche, the street urchin (*gamin*) breaks a lantern. The chapter is called 'A boy at war with street-lamps'. As the scene begins, Gavroche strays into a street where the lanterns are still burning in the middle of a rebellion. '"You've still got lights burning in these parts", he said. "That's not right, mate. No discipline. I'll have to smash it." He flung the stone, and the lamp-glass fell with a clatter which caused the occupants of the near-by houses, huddled behind their curtains, to exclaim, "It's '93 all over again!" "There you are, you old street." said Gavroche. "Now you've got your nightcap on."'[72] If light represents the order of the old society, then darkness is the counter-order of the rebellion — this is the lesson drawn from the Paris revolts in *Les Misérables*. It is elaborated in another scene, in which the young hero Marius leaves the part of Paris where normal conditions prevail and goes to the area held by the insurgents. His path takes him from light to darkness. The closer he gets to the rebel area, the darker it gets. 'At the end of

70. *Les barricades immortelles*. . . . , p. 130.
71. Quoted from Schnitzler, *Ausführlicher Bericht eines Augenzeugen*, p. 54.
72. Victor Hugo, *Les Misérables*, translated by Norman Denny (Harmondsworth, Middlesex, 1986), p. 978.

the Rue des Bourdonnais the street-lamps ceased.' This is where the no-man's-land begins, and it is completely dark. From a bird's-eye view — Hugo's favourite perspective on the city — it presents itself as

> a huge patch of darkness in the centre of Paris, a black gulf. Owing to the breaking of street-lamps and the shuttering of windows, no light was to be seen there, nor was any sound of life or movement to be heard. The invisible guardian of the uprising, that is to say, darkness, was everywhere on duty and everywhere kept order. This is the necessary tactic of insurrection, to veil smallness of numbers in a vast obscurity and enhance the stature of every combatant by the possibilities which obscurity affords. At nightfall every window where a light showed had been visited by a musket-ball; the light had gone out, and sometimes the occupant had been killed. Now nothing stirred; nothing dwelt in the houses but fear, mourning and amazement; nothing in the streets but a kind of awe-struck horror.[73]

Eighteen years later Hugo's description would not have applied. At first sight, the old, well-known scenes of lantern smashing seemed to be repeating themselves in the February Revolution of 1848. 'In the centre of Paris', writes Garnier-Pagès, chronicler of this revolution, 'the populace is destroying the *revérbères* and the gaslights. Shops are closed and dark. The darkness is total. Under its cover, armouries are being plundered and barricades erected.'[74] And Victor Hugo, this time writing as an eye-witness, not as a novelist, noted on 23 February: 'The Marais presents a dismal sight. . . . The *réverbères* are smashed and their lights extinguished'.[75] On closer inspection, however, it seems that in 1848 lanterns were not destroyed to the same extent as they had been in 1830 and in the numerous revolts of the 1830s. In any case, these two quotations are the only ones that could be found in contemporary accounts of the 1848 Revolution. But if lantern smashing was no longer what it had been, this was simply because lanterns were no longer what they had been either. Between 1830 and 1848, a technical revolu-

73. Ibid., pp. 944–5.
74. Garnier-Pagès, *Histoire de la Révolution de 1848* (Paris, 1861), Vol. 4, pp. 305–6.
75. Victor Hugo, *Choses vues* (Paris, 1913), Vol. 1, p. 310. In the same book, Hugo commented as follows on the uprising of 12 May 1839: 'The old Rue du Temple is pitch black. Here all the lanterns have been destroyed' (p. 33).

Lantern smashing in Vienna (1848).
'Flames emerged from the lower parts of the gas pipes that were still buried in the ground and flared up in red columns, lighting up the darkness of nightfall' (contemporary report).
(*Source: Genaue Darstellung der denkwürdigen Wiener Ereignisse des Jahres 1848 in ihren Ursachen und Folgen*, Vienna, 1849)

tion had taken place in the street lighting of Paris. The old oil *réverbères* had gradually been replaced by gaslights. Compared to London, this change took place very slowly in Paris. In 1830 Paris was lit exclusively by oil *réverbères*, with very few exceptions. By 1835 less than 5 per cent of the total, that is only 203 lanterns, were fed by gas. Gaslight did not become the dominant form of lighting until the 1840s, although even then, there were still many oil *réverbères* around.[76]

Owing to this new technology, street lanterns not only spread a new type of light, but they themselves — metaphorically

76. Henri Besnard, *L'Industrie du Gaz à Paris depuis ses origines*, Thèse Faculté du droit (Paris, 1942), p. 29. In 1842 there were still more oil *réverbères* than gaslights (8,000: 7,000), and even as late as 1848, when the number of gaslights had risen to 8,600, there were still almost 6,000 *réverbères* in use (ibid.).

speaking — appeared in a new light. While the individual oil lantern with its fuel reservoir was a self-contained, autonomous apparatus, the individual gaslight was part of a big industrial complex. The oil lantern was perceived to a certain extent as something individual, whose light could also be extinguished individually. Meting out the same treatment to one of the new gaslights would have been a quixotic act, for each of these was merely an offshoot of the true centre, the far distant gas-works. A new way of putting out the light, appropriate to the new technology, had to aim at shutting down the gas-works. This possibility appears as a threat for the first time in the February Revolution. Perhaps it is no coincidence that it was an American observer who found this technical change worth commenting on: 'Great anxiety was felt as night fell, relative to the gas, which it was feared would be cut off by the insurgents; but by the concentration of a large military force round the works this fear was removed, and the lamps were all lit, with the exception of those on the Champs-Elysées which had been broken by the rioters.'[77]

Unlike Paris, the other revolutionary capitals of Europe kept their street lanterns unbroken. Vienna and Berlin did not witness scenes like those that took place in Paris in July 1830 simply because they did not have a revolution then. When the spark of the February Revolution spread in 1848, street lighting remained intact — with one spectacular exception. On the night of 13 March, on the former glacis of Vienna (the area between the old city and the suburbs, which later became the 'Ring'), 'all the gas lamp-posts [were] destroyed, so that the gas flared up to the height of a man, creating a fantastic, new type of lighting in the night, one that had never been seen before.'[78]

---

77. Percy B. St. John, *The Three Days of February, 1848* (New York, 1848), p. 90. (It is conceivable that the lanterns on the Champs-Elysées were still oil *réverbères*.) In the same year, 1848, New York experienced a sudden and *simultaneous* failure of all its gaslights after an explosion in a gas-works: 'The city that night was thrown into confusion. People stumbled through darkened streets falling into holes and colliding with objects' (Louis Bader, 'Gas Illumination in New York City, 1823–1863', dissertation, New York University, 1970, p. 265).

78. Friedrich Unterreiter, *Die Revolution in Wien von März und Mai 1848* (Vienna, 1848), Vol. 1, p. 43. Here is another account of the same event: 'The iron lampposts on the glacis were all knocked over and the burning gas poured out of the pipes in a wide stream' (A. Pichler, *Aus den März- und Oktobertagen zu Wien 1848*, Innsbruck, 1850, p. 8).

The motives for this act of lantern smashing remain obscure. The light was not extinguished in order to envelop the rebels in protective darkness; on the contrary, gaslight was set free to leap up into the air as a giant flame that illuminated the night more brilliantly than any lantern. This can be chalked up to the lack of revolutionary experience that distinguished the rebels in Vienna and Berlin from those in Paris. During street fighting at night in Berlin, many windows were illuminated — not by loyal citizens who wanted to identify themselves as such to the authorities (remember the Paris police chief's appeal) but by the rebels. The commanding general describes in his memoirs how easy this made it for the advancing armed forces: 'The lights and the full moon, shining brightly in a clear sky, were a great disadvantage for the rebels. Because all the windows were illuminated, none of the shots fired by the soldiers missed, while those fired by the rebels, who were dazzled by the moonlight and by the lights in the houses opposite, were inaccurate and often went astray.'[79]

However irrational and disastrous these lights were, they completed the circle described by the revolutionary use of light. For the Paris revolutions ended not in darkness but in blazing festive illuminations. Victory — or what was perceived as victory — was celebrated in the light and with light. The street urchins who had smashed street lanterns now turned out in force to activate the new lighting. Garnier-Pagès writes: 'Gangs, consisting mainly of street urchins, roamed the streets and forced residents to illuminate their houses immediately. People obeyed this command either willingly, or most reluctantly, with much grinding of teeth. The well-known cry of "Lampions! Lampions!" rang out in voices of all pitches until a dazzling brightness satisfied this demand.'[80] The same picture emerges for Vienna: 'The people celebrated their victory with impressive torchlight processions and magnificent illuminations — no window in the city or the suburbs remained dark, it was unprecedented splendour — it was a genuine expression of joy.'[81] And in Berlin

79. Quoted from Adolf Wolff, *Berliner Revolutions-Chronik* (Berlin, 1851), Vol. 1, p. 169.
80. Garnier-Pagès, *Histoire de la Révolution*, Vol. 6, pp. 299–300.
81. Unterreiter, *Die Revolution in Wien*, p. 91.

the victory of the people was celebrated at night with a magnificent illumination; people were firing off guns with joy all night long. . . . The American envoy, Donelson, took part in the illumination with warm enthusiasm. . . . A gang of armed burghers and workers turned up at the Russian legation, too, demanding that it be lit up. Meyrendorff agreed, not exactly willingly, but the consequences of a refusal would have been serious.[82]

In the eyes of the police, these festivals of light soon became as threatening as the darkness that had preceded them. After all, these lights were neither surveillance lights nor lights of royal displays as in the festive illuminations of the *ancien régime* — they were a revival of the ancient bonfire. Thus the following public announcement appeared on 17 March in Vienna: 'As the residents of Vienna have for several days displayed their delight at the rights conceded to them by His Majesty by means of general rejoicing and illuminations, in response to a general desire we ask that, in order to avoid any disturbances and to restore the peace at night, no illuminations take place in the city and the suburbs from today on.'[83]

A Flood of Light

The flowers are real, and the trees are of
lively green . . . every dress and hat stands
out clear and sharp in its true colours as by
daylight . . . the trees and flowers are plainly
visible in every detail of leaf, petal and
twig . . . the very stones of the gravel walk,
the mosses on the walls . . . are visible.

(*The Sanitarian*, 1878)

The nineteenth century saw a radical change in public lighting. Until then, lanterns had generally cast a kind of private light; now their beams increasingly began to spread outward. Position

---

82. Veit Valentin, *Geschichte der deutschen Revolution 1848–49* (Berlin, 1930–31; reprinted Cologne, 1970), Vol. 1, p. 448.
83. Quoted from Unterreiter, *Die Revolution in Wien*, p. 96.

markers and luminous symbols of sovereignty turned into something that actually lit up the street. As technology became more sophisticated, the pools of light around solitary lanterns grew ever larger and finally merged, creating one vast sea of light. This expansion had begun in the eighteenth century, with the *réverbères*. The introduction of gas lighting, which multiplied the level of light, gave it a further boost. When the Mall in London was illuminated by gaslight for the first time in 1807, the *Monthly Magazine* printed this description: 'The effect is beyond all dispute superior to the old method of lighting our streets. One branch of the lamps illuminated with gas affords a greater intensity of light than twenty common lamps lighted with oil. The light is beautifully white and brilliant.'[84]

Although gaslight seemed as bright as daylight compared with traditional lighting, it was not long before it, in turn, was overshadowed. The first experiments using electric light to illuminate the streets took place after 1850. Suddenly, gaslight looked as obsolete as oil-lamps had a few decades earlier. The *Allgemeine Zeitung* commented on an experiment that took place in St Petersburg in 1850: 'The light of the gas lamps appeared red and sooty, while the electric light was dazzlingly white.'[85] A newspaper carried this report on the illumination of the Rue Impériale in Lyon in 1855:

As far as the gas flames are concerned, they appear pale and dim; their light is reddish and has little impact on the surroundings. The comparison is perfectly suited to showing how unsatisfactory our present lighting is and how strong and bright electric light is. We went up and down the street several times, from one end to the other, and could read at all distances. Gas lighting had no effect whatsoever on the brightness of the street; it was not turned on at all for three evenings and nobody noticed the least difference.[86]

In the 1870s and 1880s several European capitals installed arc-lights on some of the main shopping streets, with the result that the surrounding streets, still lit by gas, seemed to be in twilight. Vienna is a good example. In 1882, electric lights were installed

---

84. *Monthly Magazine*, 1807, p. 581.
85. C. H. Hassenstein, *Das elektrische Licht* (Weimar, 1859), p. 129.
86. *Gazette de Lyon* quoted from ibid., p. 133.

Arc-lights on the Potsdamer Platz, Berlin, about 1880.
(Photo archive of the Werner-von-Siemens Institut, Munich)

The expansion of street lighting.
Two generations of street-lights are clearly visible. The arc-lights
are much brighter than the weakly glowing gaslights and are
almost twice as high (Place du Carrousel, Paris, 1885).
(*Source*: *L'Electricité*, 1885.)

Experimental use of arc-lights on the Boulevard des Italiens
(*Source*: *La Lumière électrique*, 1881.)

on the Stephansplatz and the Graben. 'Anyone who came out of one of the gas-lit side streets and entered one of the places named felt as though he were stepping unexpectedly out of a half-dark passage into a room filled with daylight.'[87]

The introduction of arc lighting for the first time made good the metaphorical description of street lanterns as artificial suns. The arc-light *was*, in fact, a small sun and the light it cast had a spectrum similar to that of daylight. In arc-light, the eye saw as it did during the day, that is with the retinal cones, while in gaslight, it saw as it did at night, with retinal rods. Stepping from an arc-lit into a gas-lit street fully activated the eye's mechanism for adapting to the dark, as a medical text written in 1880 describes:

> In the middle of the night, we emerge into the brightest daylight. Shop and street signs can be recognised clearly from across the street. We can even see the features of people's faces well from quite a distance, and what is especially remarkable, the eye accustoms itself to this intense light immediately and without the slightest strain. But this impression is misleading. As soon as we look away from the broad thoroughfare into one of the side streets, where a miserable, dim gaslight is flickering, the eye-strain begins. Here darkness reigns supreme, or rather, a weak, reddish glow, that is hardly enough to prevent collisons in the entrances of houses or on the stairs; in a word, the most wretched light prevails. The pupil dilates laboriously and the retina tries to catch the smallest ray of light. The electric lantern, by contrast, emits a powerful light which illuminates both sides of the streets, chases away the shadows, floods every corner with light, because it is reflected from the pavement and the walls of houses, and eventually dissipates into the clouds.[88]

The aim of all public lighting in the 1880s was to make the streets so bright that one could read a newspaper and see the flies on the walls of houses,[89] but the prohibitive cost of electric

---

87. *Illustrirte Zeitung*, 14 April 1882, quoted from Ernst Rebske, *Lampen, Laternen, Leuchten — Eine Historie der Beleuchtung* (Stuttgart, 1962), p. 135.

88. Poncet de Cluny, in *Progrès médical* (1880), pp. 627-8.

89. The *Allgemeine Zeitung* reported from St Petersburg in 1850 that the houses were 'so brightly illuminated that one could have seen a fly sitting on the wall, even though the houses were 300 to 400 paces from the Admiralty where the arc-lamp was situated' (quoted from Hassenstein, *Das elektrische Licht*).

Scene under incandescent lights, 1885.
(*Source: La Lamière électrique*, 1885.)

lighting limited the use of arc-light. In Europe only a few especially significant streets, squares and buildings enjoyed the benefits of arc lighting.[90] Ordinary streets remained the domain of gaslight which, to be sure, was modernised extensively in response to the competition offered by arc lighting and, in the form of incandescent gas lighting, increased its output of light fivefold.

Electric arc lighting was unsuitable for general-purpose street lighting for another reason apart from its cost: this artificial sun put out more light than the street could absorb. The problem of dazzling arose — something that had never happened before. The core of the arc-light was so bright, so like the sun, that in contrast to the flame of the gaslight, it could not be·looked at directly. Fixing arc-lamps in the positions that had been used for the old street lanterns was, therefore, ruled out. They had to hang outside the normal field of vision, in a place from which only their light was visible — that is, not *in* the street but *above* it. The higher an arc-light was placed, the better; this not only cut out the glare, but also meant that a larger area was lit up. (The development of public lighting followed the almost mathematical formula of the brighter the light, the higher the lamp-post.) Taken to its logical conclusion, this meant that the optimal position for arc lighting was a high tower from where it would illuminate a large area — for example, a whole city. And in fact, long before it was technically possible to produce the required intensity of light, more or less precise ideas existed about public lighting that would no longer be *street* lighting, but *city* lighting. In 1703, an individual named Favre submitted a proposal to the Paris Académie des Sciences. It involved putting up 'lanterns to illuminate the city at night' in the French capital. Four reflector lanterns, one for each point of the compass, were to be placed 'on top of a column or a tower, to be built at the city's highest point'. As the inventor himself had his doubts about whether

90. In Paris, they included the Place de la Concorde, the Opera and the square in front of it as well as the Avenue de l'Opéra, the Arc de Triomphe, the Place du Corps Legislatif, and the Théâtre du Châtelet; in St Petersburg, the Winter Palace and Nevski Drive. The number of arc lighting units produced by Siemens shows how rarely this type of lighting was used in public places: of the total of 1,850 arc lighting systems Siemens had installed by 1890, only eleven were for 'streets and public places', while 250 were for 'spinning and weaving mills', 226 for 'various workshops, factories, etc.', and 139 for 'offices, shops and business premises' (Rebske, *Lampen, Laternen, Leuchten*, p. 169).

The lighting tower as a symbol of power.
Monument erected by Louis XIV in the Place des Victoires, 1686
(see illustration on p. 86).
(*Source*: d'Allemagne, *Histoire du luminaire*.)

Paris could really be illuminated in this way, he added a more modest variant to his proposal, suggesting that the four lanterns 'would be even more suitable for a public square where several streets meet, if they were to be mounted in the middle of the square at medium height'.[91]

More detailed than this first recorded plan for a light tower was the proposal submitted by a certain Dondey-Dupré to the First Consul of the French Republic — that is, Napoleon — in 1799. His 'project d'un nouveau mode d'illumination pour la ville de Paris' was fully in line with the revolutionary monumentalism of that period, also expressed in the architectural plans of Ledoux and Boullé. Dondey-Dupré began by referring to the lighthouse of ancient Alexandria: 'Alexandria, one of the largest and most populous cities of the world, was illuminated by a lighthouse that was extolled as one of the seven wonders of the

Project for city illumination (1703).
The inventor suggested that these enormous street-lights should be placed
'on the top of a column or tower, to be built at the city's highest point'. The
four reflector lanterns would then 'light up the city at night'.
(*Source*: Académie des Sciences. Mémoires. Machines et Inventions, Vol. 2,
1702–12, Paris, 1735)

world.' Here a footnote provided a new interpretation of this
tower (*phare*): 'It is generally accepted that this lighthouse . . .
was intended *particularly* for navigation, but its height and the
brightness of its beacon leave no room for doubt that the city of
Alexandria lying at its base was fully illuminated by it' (original
emphasis).[92] On the basis of this redefinition of the lighthouse's
function, Dondey-Dupré suggested that 'Paris, too, can be lit up
by *gigantic* lighthouses. . . . If their height and the distance
between them is calculated exactly, then these towers will cast
an amount of light that corresponds exactly to their size and the
fuel they burn. They will therefore provide as much light as is
wanted. The main tower is to be built in the Place de la Revolution, where it will be an overwhelming sight, something like a
large conflagration. The other towers, to be built in the city's
most important squares, will provide such an interplay of light
that darkness will be totally banished. These overlapping lights

92. Dondey-Dupré, *Projet*. . . (Paris, 1799; An X), p. 4. (The only copy of this pamphlet
known to the author is in the Bibliothèque National in Paris.)

will flood Paris with light like an artificial meteor. It will not be difficult to direct the rays of light and reflect them so that *no* shadows will remain' (original emphases).[93] Dondey-Dupré proposed using the following experimental model to work out the height and number of towers required to banish shadows:

> Build several card houses of varying height. Place an adjustable candlestick in the middle of them. Now lift the light to the height at which the space between the card houses is lit up without any shadows remaining. If the light is too high in proportion, add one or more lights until all the shadows are gone. If one then measures the differences in height between the highest card house and the highest light, and makes the necessary arithmetical calculations, one can establish that if the houses are of a certain height, the lighthouse has to be a certain amount higher.[94]

For all the shrewdness of his presentation of the incidence of light and the casting of shadow as soluble problems, Dondey-Dupré did not identify the most important element in his scheme: an adequate source of light. In a secretive, alchemistic hint, he did no more than state that 'the fuel to be used by the lighthouses is *the secret of the author*, who reserves the right to announce it as soon as a public trial has taken place' (original emphasis).[95] The mysterious fuel may in fact have been nothing other than gas. Just at that time, Philippe Lebon was doing his first experiments with gas lighting, and in the same year as Dondey-Dupré announced his *projet*, Lebon published a small paper entitled 'Moyens nouveaux d'employer les combustibles plus utilement et à la chaleur et à la lumière et d'en recueillir les divers produits' (New methods for employing heating and lighting fuels more profitably and for collecting the various constituents).[96]

Whatever Dondey-Dupré's mysterious fuel, his was not the only futuristic light tower built in the nineteenth-century imagination. These other towers, which were also intended to bring a second dawn to the urban night, were to be fuelled by gas.

93. Ibid., pp. 5–6.
94. Ibid., p. 7.
95. Ibid., p. 6.
96. See Ch. 1, above.

Joseph Méry, for example, described a scheme for lighting Paris involving 100-metre-high towers, one in each *arrondissement*.[97] Théophile Gautier dreamt of 'lighting up the night with perfumed gas. . . . The light streams forth out of big towers and is brighter than daylight.'[98]

In Europe such ideas remained in the realm of Utopian literature. In the United States they became reality. The work of the inventor Benjamin Henfrey in 1802–3 was a prelude to this development. Henfrey offered to build lighting towers for several towns, but none of them took up his offer.[99] Eventually, however, he got the chance to build one of these structures. In 1802, a 13-metre-high tower (about 40 feet) was erected according to his instructions in Richmond, the capital of Virginia. A thermolamp, modelled on Lebon's, was placed on top of it. Never more than a passing attraction, this tower cannot have been much brighter than an ordinary nautical lighthouse. 'Large crowds came at first to view the light, but as time went on, enthusiasm lessened. The tower was soon abandoned and Richmond reverted to the use of lamp posts lit by oil.'[100]

When the discovery of electric arc-light finally made it possible to produce the quantities and intensities of light required, many American towns, especially in the mid-West and the West, installed 'tower lighting'. From towers or masts that varied in height from 50 to 150 metres (about 150 to 450 feet)[101] a powerful light flooded the town. A deeply impressed French observer described the sight in 1885: 'Electric light inundates the whole town and penetrates right into the outlying districts, which, until then, did not even have a single gaslight.'[102]

Detroit — 'the only large city in the world lighted wholly by

97. Citron, *La poésie de Paris*, Vol. 2, p. 123.

98. Quoted from ibid.

99. In 1802 Henfrey suggested to the City Council of Baltimore that it should erect 'tall towers with strong lights acting as beacons which would serve to illuminate the surrounding areas' (Bader, 'Gas Illumination in New York City', p. 42). One year later he submitted a similar proposal to the City Council of Philadelphia: 'Towers were to be erected in certain parts of the city so that their lights cast from a great height would serve to illuminate entire areas of streets and alleys' (ibid., p. 44).

100. Ibid., pp. 43–4.

101. *La Lumière électrique*, 21 February 1885, p. 341; *L'Electricité* (1882), p. 141; ibid. (1885), p. 28.

102. Ibid. (1885), p. 30. This refers to the city lighting of San José in California, which consisted of 60-metre-high towers.

American lighting tower, San José, California, 1885
(*Source*: *L'Electricité*, 1885)

the tower system'[103] — provides a good example of an integrated tower lighting system. One hundred and twenty-two towers lit up the 54 square kilometres (21 square miles) covered by the city. Each one of these towers was about 50 metres (153 feet) high. The distance between them varied from 350 to 400 metres in the city centre to 1,000 metres in the outlying districts.[104] Consequently, the intensity of the light varied.

Gradations in the brightness of street lighting were, of course, nothing new. Since the beginnings of public lighting, there had always been more lanterns in important thoroughfares and shopping streets than in side streets. But in traditional street lighting, the intensity of light varied from street to street. Dimly lit side streets led off brightly lit shopping streets. Tower lighting, by contrast, created districts or belts of light that bore no relation to individual streets. They simply laid themselves over the town like a uniform carpet of light. This light was as invariable as the chequered pattern of the streets that it illuminated. Two totally rationalised and geometrically divided surfaces matched and complemented each other; cities lit in this way were like living Utopias of equality. This was, in fact, one of the main arguments put forward in favour of this type of lighting. The City Council Committee of Flint (Michigan) justified its decision to introduce a tower lighting system by pointing out

that this is a system by which not only the streets, but the alleys, railroad crossings, depots, bridges, and even private grounds, are equally well lighted . . . and it matters not how many streets are opened, or houses built within the district [of a light tower], the light covers the entire space. . . . We claim for it that it may be justly called the poor man's light, for, by reason of its penetrating and far-reaching rays, the suburbs of the city will be equally well lighted with the more central portions, and instead of a feeble flicker of the gasoline lamps, a clear and brilliant light will penetrate the most distant parts of the city.[105]

American tower lighting turned out to be a mere episode in the history of lighting. Thirty years after its installation, De-

103. Fred H. Whipple, *Municipal Lighting* (Detroit, 1888), p. 157.
104. Ibid.
105. Quoted from ibid., pp. 162–3.

troit's tower lighting system was dismantled and replaced by 'regular' street lighting. 'The old system of tower lighting', wrote a chronicler of Detroit five years later, 'was more spectacular than efficient.' The same light that thirty years earlier had been admired as a triumph of technology and democracy was now seen to be inadequate and dysfunctional. 'A twilight glow was shed over a wide area', continues the same chronicler, 'but there was no effective lighting anywhere.'[106] It turned out that for public lighting to be effective, it had to relate to the street after all — it needed to be street lighting. But the notion of lighting up whole cities or parts of cities uniformly from above proved to be an *idée fixe* of the sort that are produced now and then when technology offers new opportunities. If these are pursued to their logical conclusion, the result is often something that can be called technical monumentalism, in contrast to the practical applications of a particular technology. In the creation of such structures, technical rationality overshoots the mark and ends up in the realms of technical fantasy and pipe dreams. (The boundaries to art often become indistinct in such cases, as the Eiffel Tower shows.) American lighting towers were in some respects a manifestation of this sort of technical monumentalism, but they also represented a technical solution to the problem of lighting that was appropriate to the specific conditions of America — they were practical, functional and, above all, economical. In a country where wages were considerably higher than in Europe, it was simply cheaper in terms of labour to build one high tower than to put up hundreds of lampposts. And European visitors often commented on *how* cheaply and functionally these towers were constructed: 'In the United States the towers have not been designed with any pretense to anything like unobtrusive plainness, for they are ugly ironmongery looking things, with the most defiant appearance of utter disregard for every other claim except utility.'[107]

Back in Europe, tower lighting remained a Utopian fantasy, and electric arc lighting changed nothing in this respect. But in one case it inspired a project of such monumentalism that this alone justifies having a closer look at it. The scene was Paris; let us return to the monument described in the first chapter.

106. George B. Catlin, *The Story of Detroit* (Detroit, 1923), p. 608.
107. *Electrical Engineer* (London), February 1885, p. 129.

The Sun Tower

In the early 1880s a French electrical engineer called Sébillot set out on a tour of the United States, an almost obligatory part of a technical education in those days. Of all the installations he visited, it was the lighting towers that captured his imagination most vividly. On returning to Paris, he began thinking about trying out something similar himself. He found a soulmate and interested partner in the architect Jules Bourdais, who had just made a name for himself by building the Trocadéro. Soon after, the committee preparing the 1889 Exposition launched a competition for a monumental landmark, and Sébillot and Bourdais entered their project. This was, to quote the title of Bourdais' submission, a 'Colonne-Soleil, Project de Phare électrique de 360 mètres de hauteur destiné à éclairer tout Paris. Construction monumentale'[108] (a 'Sun Tower, an electric lighthouse, 360 metres high, to light up the whole of Paris. A monumental construction'). Or, in Sébillot's words: 'Avant-Projet d'éclairage de la ville de Paris par un seul foyer lumineux'[109] (' . . . a project to light up Paris from a single source of light'). Bourdais was to take responsibility for the architecture, Sébillot for the lighting engineering. The Sun Tower, along with another project involving a tower, that of the bridge construction engineer Gustave Eiffel, made the committee's short list. Its pros and cons were discussed in detail at the meetings of the Société des Ingénieurs Civils de France, and it attracted a great deal of attention in the French and European technical press. In the end, the Eiffel Tower won the competition, not because it was thought to be impossible to light Paris centrally from the Sun Tower, but because it seemed too expensive, impractical and dangerous. But the fact that Eiffel, too, considered putting an arc lighting system on top of his tower shows how attractive the idea was.[110]

108. *Société des ingénieurs civils de France, Mémoires et compte rendu des travaux, Année 1885*, Vol. 1, p. 53.

109. Ibid., p. 73.

110. During the Exposition, the Eiffel Tower was intended 'to carry an electric light that would illuminate the entire exhibition ground', reported the *Wochenschrift des Österreichischen Ingenieur- und Architekten-Vereins* (1886, no. 49, p. 395). Further, it was not ruled out that, 'as has long been planned, all the streets of Paris could be illuminated from this one, high, central source'.

The Sun Tower (1885).
(*Source: Société des ingénieurs civils. Mémoires et compte rendu des travaux*, Paris, 1885)

In style, the projected Sun Tower was traditional, as was the planned building material: it was to be a massive granite column with a diameter of sixteen metres, resting on a cubic pedestal 66 metres (216 feet) high and also made of stone. The shaft of the column was to be decorated with an iron construction in a historical style that gave the whole thing a certain similarity with the Leaning Tower of Pisa.[111] Sébillot, the engineer, would have preferred a more modern structure, someting like the Eiffel Tower: 'I had originally thought of an iron structure', he confessed, 'but Monsieur Bourdais, to whom I told my plans, disagreed. In a city like Paris, he said, the "torch-bearer" had to be more artistic, especially as it was so novel a monument and was to fulfil such functions. Apart from that, he argued, a public monument of this nature had to have a longer life-span'.[112]

The Sun Tower was intended to do more than just provide light. The 66-metre-high pedestal was to house a museum of electricity; the top of the tower was to hold a viewing platform for 1,000 visitors. In between, in the shaft of the column, there were to be lifts as well as 'an absolutely empty cylinder with a diameter of 8 metres, that could be used for all manner of scientific experiments — for example, to test the free fall of objects, the compression of gas and steam, the Foucault pendulum, etc'.[113] In addition, there would be space for eighty rooms where patients could receive air therapy. A monumental statue, representing an allegory of the spirit of science, was to crown the structure.

The place selected for the Sun Tower was the topographical centre of Paris, the area around the Pont Neuf. From here, the arc-light to be installed at the top of the tower — at the feet of the allegory of science — was to illuminate Paris within a radius of 5.5 kilometres (3.5 miles),[114] not directly, but by means of a big reflector above the actual arc-light that would spread the

111. According to Bourdais' submission (See *Société des ingenieurs*, Vol. 1, p. 53).

112. See *Société des ingenieurs*, Vol. 1, p. 74.

113. See ibid., p. 71.

114. *La Lumiére électrique* (21 February 1885, p. 340) described the system thus: 'The lanterns are distributed around the rim of the reflector, in a circle with a diameter of 12 metres and a circumference of 36 metres. If every lantern takes up thirty-six centimeters of space, then the reflector can hold 100 high-powered lights. According to Monsieur Sébillot's calculations, every lamp has an output of 20,000 Carcel. The total output is therefore 2 million Carcel.'

Project for city illumination (1882).
The Partz System for illuminating Paris involved erecting several
lighting towers throughout the metropolitan area. The light
source, a powerful arc-light, was to be located under the street.
Strong reflectors at the top of the towers would disseminate the
light.
(*Source*: *La Lumière électrique*, 1882.)

light over a wide area. Additional reflectors throughout Paris would cast the light of this artificial sun into the most distant corners; it would, in Sébillot's words, 'penetrate inside houses and flats', like real sunlight.[115]

There is no need to go into the technical arguments with which contemporary lighting engineers pulled this plan to pieces — they are obvious. The main objection, of course, was that especially in the more distant districts, the light would dazzle rather than illuminate.[116] If Paris were to have this sort of monumental city lighting at all, several counter-proposals suggested, then it would have to follow the American model and consist of several towers distributed throughout the city— for example, four towers as high as the Eiffel Tower, or 100 towers of 60 to 80 metres (about 200 to 250 feet) in height.[117] A number of towers seemed a better idea for security reasons as well, since a technical breakdown in one tower would not necessarily affect the lighting of the whole city. And finally, memories stirred of rebels smashing lanterns. As in February 1848 when the rebels seemed to be threatening the gas-works, it was now feared 'that the Sun Tower could one day become the target of attacks by rebels, who might seize it instead of the Town Hall. The Tower would have to be protected against such an attack'.[118] The Sun Tower that aroused such fears was itself perhaps nothing but an attempt to prevent any further revolutions — indeed, to nip any such idea in the bud — by flooding the city with light. Fifteen years after the Commune, the biggest nineteenth-century revolutionary trauma for the French bourgeoisie, this motive was not totally irrelevant, even if it remained a subconscious one. (Similarly, one could interpret the Sun Tower's shape — a heroic, monumental column — as a reaction to the Communards' destruction of the Vêndome column.)

Public lighting that could illuminate a city as completely as the Sun Tower should have done, was an old Utopian dream. Mercier's late-eighteenth-century vision of Paris in the year 2440

---

115. See *Société des ingénieurs*, Vol. 1, p. 78.

116. 'Even if the light were strong enough to penetrate right to the edges of the area, no one would appreciate it. Everybody would turn away from the light tower, dazzled, and its presence would be regarded as offensive' (*Electro-technische Zeitschrift*, March 1887, p. 122).

117. Ibid.; See also *Société des ingénieurs*, Vol. 1, p. 656.

118. See *Société des ingénieurs*, Vol. 1, p. 639.

Lighting tower at the International Electricity Exhibition, Paris, 1881.
(*Source*: *L'Illustration*, 1881)

has street lights so bright that 'their combined impact left no shadows at all'. The only conceivable consequence, for Mercier, was an improvement in public morals: 'On the street corners there were no more prostitutes with painted faces and one foot in the gutter, offering their coarse and vulgar pleasures in the language of soldiers, accompanied by brazen looks and obscene gestures.'[119]

In the course of the nineteenth century, the value placed on

119. Louis Sébastien Mercier, *Paris l'an 2440* (Paris, 1977), p. 147. (This quotation is taken from the chapter 'Les lanternes'.)

light as a guarantor of public morals, safety and order decreased as lights actually became brighter. One of the first people to see that a room in shadowless light offered a new kind of threat was Jules Michelet. In 1845 he wrote about gaslight in the new factories: 'These newly built big halls, flooded by brilliant light, torture eyes accustomed to darker quarters. Here there is no darkness, into which thought can withdraw, here there are no shadowy corners in which the imagination can indulge its dreams. No illusion is possible in this light. Incessantly and mercilessly, it brings us back to reality.'[120] The twentieth century was to experience this relentless light to the full. The glaring and shadowless light that illuminates H.G. Wells' negative Utopias,[121] no longer guarantees the security of the individual. It permits total surveillance by the state. The Utopian dream of nights lit up as bright as day was transformed into the nightmare of a light from which there was no escape. 'A new sort of urban star now shines out nightly, horrible, unearthly, obnoxious to the human eye' — this is Robert Louis Stevenson's description of electric arc lighting. 'A lamp for a nightmare! Such a light as this should shine only on murders and public crime, or along the corridors of lunatic asylums, a horror to heighten horror.'[122]

---

120. Jules Michelet, *Le Peuple* (Paris, 1974), p. 100.

121. For example, H.G. Wells, *When the Sleeper Wakes*: 'Overhead mighty cantilevers sprang together across the huge width of the place, and a tracery of translucent material shut out the sky. Gigantic globes of cool white light shamed the pale sunbeams that filtered down through the girders and wires' (quoted from Mark R. Hillegas, *The Future as Nightmare: H.G. Wells and the Anti-Utopians*, New York, 1967, p. 43).

122. Robert Louis Stevenson, 'A Plea for Gas Lamps', in *The Travels and Essays* (New York, 1917), Vol. 13, pp. 168–9. In this context, it is interesting to look at the military uses to which arc lighting was put. During the 1880s, especially in colonial wars, arc lighting was as successful as European firearms had been in the sixteenth century. An English fleet off Alexandria 'uses several arc-lamps every night, directing their light on to the city and the surrounding coastal areas — to the great dismay of the Egyptian soldiers, who assume that supernatural forces are at work in this, to them, totally puzzling phenomenon' (*La Lumière électrique*, vol. 6, 1882, p. 566).

Night Life

On se promène, on flâne dans toutes ces
rues, où le commerce entretient tous les soirs
une illumination splendide.

(Julien Lemer, *Paris au gaz*, 1861)

In the seventeenth century the two frontiers of the night —
previously *terra incognita* — were discovered and thrown open at
once. The police conquered and controlled the night by installing street lighting. Simultaneously with this *lighting of order*, a
lighting of festivity developed in the form of baroque festivals of
light and firework displays. 'There is no more brilliant spectacle,
and none that is more popular at public celebrations', wrote
Michel de Pure in his *Idée des Spectacles Anciens et Nouveaux*
(1688). 'In almost all nations it serves to express joy at a great
victory.'[1]

Using fire to express joy is an ancient custom. In its oldest
form, it was a bonfire — usually a pyre that burned itself out in a
wild blaze of light. Here fire, destruction and illumination
merged to create an engulfing and complex experience that far
exceeded that of simple brightness. The archaic bonfire could be
described as a saturnalian version of the hearth fire: an out-
pouring of ecstasy as everyday restraints were suddenly lifted.
Festive illuminations and fireworks replaced the bonfire, culti-
vating, ordering and disciplining its wild power. Thousands of
candles and fireworks formed precisely calculated geometric
patterns, a glowing transcription of court ceremonial into light,
executed by a fireworks' master to display the brilliance of his
sovereign's rule. None the less, these displays retained some of
the pyromaniacal satisfactions of the original bonfire, so much
so that in seventeenth-century France they were still known by
the same name: *Feux de Joye*. After all, they consisted of balls of
fire, showers of sparks and wonderfully exploding rockets — in
short, a continuously changing spectacle of blazing light, just
like a bonfire. Even when illuminations and fireworks had
become aestheticised, the primeval power of fire would some-

1. Michel de Pure, *Idée des Spectacles Anciens et Nouveaux* (Paris, 1668; reprint Geneva 1972),
p. 183.

times flare up in an unintended firework display.[2]

Spectacles of light were part of the festive culture of the baroque period. They lit up celebrations held at night — probably the most significant innovation of baroque courtly culture. In the Middle Ages and during the Renaissance, festivities had taken place in broad daylight. Now they began after sunset. 'At 8 or 9 the theatre starts, at midnight there is a supper . . . followed by dancing to daybreak. And when the coaches leave the court to go home at dawn, they meet the burghers in the streets, just going to work.'[3] Richard Alewyn's description hints at the motives behind this shift in the time of festivities. To enjoy oneself while working people slept and to go to bed when artisans and burghers were just starting their working day reversed the normal order of things. It was a social privilege that gave the evening's entertainment extra spice. Added to this were the qualities and states that, since time immemorial, had been associated with night as the antithesis of day: at night, regions that remained closed to people during the day were open to them; night-time brought one into a more direct relationship with the cosmos; it dissolved fixed forms and blurred the distinctions between reality and fantasy. When the night was magically lit up during a festive illumination the removal from reality — almost as if through the effects of a drug — was complete. The 'scene of a second, symbolic life', as Alewyn puts it, was created.

The baroque culture of the night spawned modern night life, which, since its conception in the cities of eighteenth-century Europe, has grown into a characteristic feature of present-day urban life. It began around 1700 in England with the creation of pleasure gardens such as Vauxhall and Ranelagh. They are best

2. 'In France, the connection between the bonfire and fireworks remained alive for a long time. As late as the eighteenth century, Midsummer Day was celebrated with a 'Feu de joye complet', that is with a bonfire plus fireworks, in every French town with any claim to significance. And in Paris around the middle of the eighteenth century a rough pyramid of wood would be piled up next to the elaborate edifice for the fireworks in front of the Hôtel de Ville on Midsummer Eve and lit, just as a bonfire had been lit on this day in ancient times to celebrate the summer solstice' (ibid, p. 57). In the perfected firework displays of the baroque period, the edifice from which the fireworks were let off took over the function of the bonfire. 'At the end, the beautiful monument that had served its purpose was burnt, together with the boats that had carried it, in a huge bonfire that rounded off the festive day' (Lotz, p. 61, describing a floating firework display at Versailles in 1674).

3. Richard Alewyn, *Das Große Welttheater* (Hamburg, 1959), p. 31.

Firework display, Stuttgart, 1616.
The origin of the baroque firework display in the medieval
bonfire is clearly visible here in Merian's illustration. The
fireworks were let off from a wooden edifice, built in the shape
of a ship, which can be described as an artistically refined and
stylised version of the pyre. These wooden constructions
themselves were always burned at the end of the firework
display.
(Archiv für Kunst und Geschichte.)

described as commercial imitations of courtly festive culture. The entertainments on offer — for the price of an admission ticket — included concerts, illumination and fireworks. Food and drink were available, and sometimes there was dancing. Although these gardens were open during the day, they only really came alive at night — at Vauxhall, between 6 and 8 o'clock. As the years passed, these times were pushed back further and further.[4] 'The present folly is late hours', remarked Horace Walpole in 1777. 'Everybody tries to be particular by being too late, and as everybody tries it, nobody is so. It is the fashion now to go to Ranelagh two hours after it is "over".'[5] In the eighteenth century, this was not merely a passing fashion; it was part of a wider movement.

Court society had underlined the distance that separated it from the bourgeoisie by ostentatiously keeping late hours, day and night. Now the middle classes tried to distance themselves from the petty bourgeoisie and the artisan class in the same way. The later one began the day, the higher one's social rank. Consequently, everything began to happen later and later. Since then, getting up early and going to bed early has become the mark of a simple life. Getting up late, getting to the office late (perhaps staying there late into the evening hours as well), taking late meals and, after an extended *soirée* (instead of simply 'knocking off work', like the lower classes), going to bed late — this has come to characterise the better social circles. What has happened to mealtimes makes this clear, as in the following description of Paris customs in 1801:

Two hundred years ago, Parisians ate their main meal [dinner] at 12 o'clock midday; today, the artisan eats at 2 p.m., the merchant at 3 and the clerk at 4; the *nouveau riche*, entrepreneurs and bill brokers at 5; Ministers, Deputies and rich bachelors at 6. The latter normally finish their dinner at the hour when our fathers used to sit down to their evening meal. Three-quarters of Parisians no longer eat at night; half of them have adopted this custom for reasons of economy.

4. Warwick Wroth, *The London Pleasure Gardens of the 18th Century* (London, 1896), p. 305. These times apply to the second half of the eighteenth century. Before 1760, concerts began around 6 or 7 p.m. (ibid., p. 303).

5. Quoted from Walter Sidney Scott, *Green Retreats: The Story of Vauxhall Gardens 1661-1859* (London, 1955), p. 15.

Vauxhall Gardens in the evening
(Illustration by George Cruikshank, Science
Museum, London.)

Those who do eat an evening meal start at 11 p.m. and go to bed
when the workers rise.[6]

At the time of Louis XIV, theatres began between 4 and 7 p.m.;
in the eighteenth century, the starting time of 5.15 p.m.
became established. Performances finished around 9 p.m.[7] The
late hours that we know from Balzac's novels did not become
customary until after the Revolution. The theatre or the opera
were followed by supper, or a visit to a casino, a ball or a
brothel. The evening usually ended at about three o'clock in the

6. Jean Baptiste Pujoulx, *Paris à la fin du 18ᵉ siècle* (Paris, 1801), pp. 141–2; see also
Wolfgang Nahrstedt, *Die Entstehung der Freizeit, dargestellt am Beispiel Hamburgs* (Göttingen,
1971), pp. 115ff and 186ff.
7. Gösta Bergman, *Lighting in the Theatre* (Stockholm, 1977), pp. 144 and 149; Mercier,
Tableau de Paris, Vol. 3, p. 88.

morning, when the revellers on their way home met the first
workers going about their business.[8]

This new order of the day — or rather, of the night — marked
not only the social gulf between the leisured classes and the
working population, but also the difference between the metropolis and the provinces. In the early nineteenth century, German travellers, princes and artisans alike, frequently expressed
their surprise at how late Paris and London remained awake.
'The opera does not finish until after 1 a.m.', Prince Pückler
reported from London to his home in Saxony, 'one rarely gets
home before 3 or 4 a.m. . . . But then high society does not
come alive again before 2 p.m.'[9] But the elevated circles in which
high-ranking people such as Pückler moved were not the only
ones that stayed awake and lively so long; so did the commercial
and amusement centres of the masses: 'Warehouses and shops
mostly stay open until midnight, but then they usually do not
open until 9 a.m. . . . The day, for business or entertainment,
really lasts until midnight; not until then does some peace — in
some quarters, total peace — descend.'[10]

What we think of as night life includes this nocturnal round of
business, pleasure and illumination. It derives its own, special
atmosphere from the light that falls onto the pavements and
streets from shops (especially those selling luxury goods), cafés
and restaurants, light that is intended to attract passers-by and
potential customers. It is advertising light — commercialised
festive illumination — in contrast to street light, the lighting of a
policed order. Commercial light is to police light what bourgeois
society is to the state. As the state, in its appropriately named
'night-watchman' function, guarantees the security that bourgeois society needs to pursue its business interests, so public
lighting creates the framework of security within which commercial lighting can unfold. When shop lights go out after
business hours, the light of the street lanterns, whose weak

8. This is how books on night life generally finished. They were published mainly in the
1850s and 1860s — for example, Julien Lemer, *Paris au gaz* (1861), Alfred Delvau, *Les Heures
parisiennes* (1866), and Julius Rodenberg, *Paris bei Sonnenschein und Lampenlicht* (1867).

9. *Fürst Pückler reist nach England. Aus den Briefen eines Verstorbenen* (Stuttgart, n.d.), pp.
144–5.

10. August Jäger, *Der Deutsche in London. Ein Beitrag zur Geschichte der politischen Flüchtlinge
unserer Zeit* (Leipzig, 1839), 2 vols. in one, pp. 188–9.

glimmer was drowned in the sea of advertising lights, becomes visible again and the lanterns go into action as the guardians of order that they have always been.

Unlike police lighting, which is uniform and homogeneous, ✓ commercial light is fed by heterogeneous sources. That is why, even today, it lends the city colour. Commercial lighting began in shops, and it still draws the bulk of its light from them.

Shop Windows

Until the late seventeenth century, shops for retail trade were little more than anterooms of the warehouses behind them. Indeed, their plain and simple furnishings made them almost indistinguishable from warehouses. But they compensated for their austerity with magnificent signboards, which hung out in the street showing what was on sale. When it was discovered, during the seventeenth and eighteenth centuries, that the signboards obstructed the traffic, these imaginative precursors of modern advertising gradually disappeared from the streets. As Sombart comments, 'the disappearance of these signboards, one after the other, almost as symbols of a dying age, was one of those momentous steps out of the cheerful world of words and colours into the grey world of figures'.[11] But this is only half the story. The colourful and aesthetic display of shop signs disappeared from the streets only to reappear, in a different form, inside the shop. A new combination of aesthetics and business was developing in the capitals of Europe. The luxury trade was in the hands of bourgeois merchants, but their customers were almost exclusively members of the court aristocracy. In the cities, the trade in luxury goods depended almost entirely on the court. To quote Sombart again: 'The elegant luxury shops, in particular, which had multiplied in Paris and London since the seventeenth century, served as popular meeting places for high society, for people who were happy to spend an hour of the day there, chatting, looking at the newest goods available and buy-

11. Werner Sombart, *Der moderne Kapitalismus* (1st edn, Munich, 1902), Vol. 2, p. 402.

ing a few things, rather like at fashionable art auctions today.'[12]

The new social role of shops was reflected in their interior design. Catering for the taste of their customers, shop owners made their sales-rooms look like reception rooms in a palace. The most popular materials were rare woods, marble, brass and especially the high-status materials used at Court: glass and mirrors.

The new splendour was foreign to the bourgeois, puritan morality of traders who experienced this transformation in the early eighteenth century. 'It is a modern custom, and wholly unknown to our ancestors, who yet understood trade, in proportion to the Business they carried on, as well as we do, to have tradesmen lay out two-thirds of their fortune in fitting up their shops', writes Defoe in *The Complete Tradesman*.

> By fitting up, I do not mean furnishing their shops with wares and goods to sell; for in that they came up to us in every particular, and perhaps beyond us too; but in painting and gilding, in fine shelves, shutters, boxes, glass doors, sashes and the like, in which they tell us now, 'tis a small matter to lay out two hundred or three hundred pounds, nay five hundred pounds to fit up a Pastry-Cook's, or a Toy-Shop. The first inference to be drawn from this must necessarily be, that this age must have more fools than the last, for certainly fools only are most taken with shews and outsides . . ., but that a fine shew of shelves and glass windows should bring customers, that was never made a rule in trade till now.[13]

As an example of a luxurious fitting-out, Defoe refers to a pastry shop in which £300 was spent on furnishings, while the stock was only worth £20. Defoe's description is one of the very few that have survived from the early period of the luxury trade:

1. Sash windows, all of looking-glass plates, 12 inches by 16 inches in measure.
2. All the walks of the shops lin'd up with galley tiles, and the

---

12. Ibid., p. 463; see also Sombart's study, *Kapitalismus und Luxus*. In it, he argues that the court aristocracy's consumption of luxury goods ruined it financially while at the other end of the same process, the bourgeoisie's role as supplier of luxury goods was the thing that allowed the bourgeois economy to begin to blossom.

13. Daniel Defoe, *The Complete Tradesman*, 2nd edn (London, 1727; reprinted New York, 1969), Vol. 1, pp. 257–8.

Shop window illuminated by gaslight (about 1870)
(Archiv für Kunst und Geschichte.)

Back-shop with galley-tiles in pannels, finely painted in forest-work and figures.
3. Two large Peir looking-glasses and one chimney glass in the shop, and one very large Peir-glass seven foot high in the Back-shop.
4. Two large branches of Candlesticks, one in the shop and one in the back-room.
5. Three great glass Lanthorns in the shop, and eight small ones.
6. Twenty-five sconces against the wall, with a large pair of silver standing candlesticks in the back room.[14]

The glass, mirrors and lights used in its furnishing must have made this shop a remarkably sparkling, reflecting, brilliant room — a miniature hall of mirrors.[15] In Defoe's time, all this splen-

14. Ibid., p. 259.
15. The use of large mirrors in seventeenth-century palaces has been explained as an

dour was limited to the interior of the shop. This changed with the social profile of the customers, as increasingly anonymous buyers replaced what had been a largely personal clientele. The more the streets could supply potential customers, the more the shops opened up to them. The display window, that began to develop as an independent part of the shop around the middle of the eighteenth century, was the scene of this interchange. While previously it had been little more than an ordinary window that permitted people to see into and out of the shop, it now became a glassed-in stage on which an advertising show was presented. 'Behind the great glass windows absolutely everything one can think of is neatly and attractively displayed in such abundance of choice as almost to make one greedy', wrote Sophie von La Roche from London in the 1780s. 'There is a cunning device for showing women's materials. They hang down in folds behind the fine, high windows so that the effect of this or that material, as it would be in a woman's dress, can be studied.'[16]

In the eighteenth and nineteenth centuries, shop display windows still looked like ordinary windows. They consisted not of a single sheet of glass, but of several smaller panes, separated by a number of ribs. Around 1850 it became technically possible to produce large sheets of glass and so to have a glass shop-front which presented 'an uninterrupted mass of glass from the ceiling to the ground', as an observer pointed out admiringly in 1851.[17] This had a profound impact on the appearance of the wares on display. The uninterrupted, transparently sparkling surface acted rather like glass on a framed painting. 'Dull colours receive . . . an element of freshness, sparkle and refinement, because glass as a medium alters appearances and irritates the eye' — this is how Hirth explains the phenomenon. He adds in a footnote: 'Putting paintings under glass makes

---

attempt to create *an illusion of space*. 'High walls, doors, even ceilings are more and more often covered with mirrors. Their purpose, however, is not to reflect any particular, delimited image, but to give the impression of a scintillating, rather kaleidoscopic and uncertain sum of light and decoration' (Georg Hirth, *Das deutsche Zimmer der Gotik und Renaissance, des Barock- Rokoko- und Zopfstils* (Munich and Leipzig, 1899), p. 154.

16. Quoted from Dorothy Davis, *A History of Shopping* (London and Toronto, 1966), p. 192.

17. Charles Knight (1851), quoted from Alison Adburgham, *Shops and Shopping 1800-1914* (London, 1964), p. 96.

Night life. 'Shops, right up to first-floor level, were as resplendent as fantasy palaces: gold, finery, jewels, flowers, cloth, carpets, bronze and vases sparkled brilliantly for sale. And the pavements in front of the theatres and cafés were full of people strolling in the mild winter night.' (Description of life on the paris boulevards late in the evening, 1849.)
(*Source*: *La Lumière électrique*, 1881)

them appear better than they really are. The protective glass confers upon good copies an additional element of deception. The plate glass of shop windows, too, has an "improving" effect on some goods.'[18]

Artificial light also helped to make the wares on display look more attractive. Its importance grew as business hours were extended into the late evening. During a visit to London in 1775, Lichtenberg observed how shops drew attention to their win-

18. Hirth, *Das deutsche Zimmer*, p. 152. Albert Smith gives us a good example of what a glance through such a window revealed: 'How richly falls the drapery of those emblazoned shawls through the fair plate-glass. How the rows of loves of bonnets. . . gladden and sadden at the same moment the bright female eyes . . . . How gorgeously shines the plate' (*Sketches of London Life and Character*, London, 1859, p. 117, quoted from Wilfried B. Whitaker, *Victorian and Edwardian Shopworkers*, Newton Abbot, 1973, p. 31).

dows by special effects with coloured lights: 'Apothecaries and grocers display glasses . . . filled with coloured spirits and cover large areas with crimson, yellow, verdigris and skyblue light. Confectioners dazzle the eye with their chandeliers and tickle the nose with their wares at no greater effort or cost than turning both in their direction.'[19] Berlin pastry cooks displayed in their windows 'artificially lit scenes, populated by small, three-dimensional figures, often artificially animated, the whole thing resembling a diorama'. In fact, these displays are thought to have inspired the development of the diorama.[20] Mostly, however, shop window lighting followed the path taken by stage lighting. As long as lights were too weak to be used indirectly, that is with the aid of reflectors, they were placed among the goods in the window. When gas and electricity increased the range over which light could be cast, the source of the light itself disappeared from view. Around the middle of the nineteenth century gaslights on London shops were 'fixed outside the shop, with a reflector so placed as to throw a strong light upon the commodities in the window'.[21] The introduction of electric light, which was not a fire hazard and therefore no longer had to be installed outside the display window, finally made it possible to achieve the sort of lighting effects that were used on the stage. A 1926 advertising handbook states that shop windows should not be 'evenly lit up. Individual spots and objects are to be highlighted by means of strong, concealed reflectors'.[22]

The illuminated window as stage, the street as theatre and the passers-by as audience — this is the scene of big-city night life. As the boulevard at night developed in the nineteenth century, it did in fact look like an interior out of doors. 'Always festively illuminated, golden cafés, a stylish and elegant throng, dandies,

---

19. Letter to Boie, 10 January 1775, in *Lichtenbergs Werke in einem Band* (Stuttgart, 1924), pp. 356–7.

20. Marianne Mildenberger, *Film und Projektion auf der Bühne* (Emsdetten, Westphalia, 1961), p. 22.

21. Charles Knight, quoted from Adburgham, *Shops and Shopping*, p. 96. 'Reflectors made of nickel silver or mirror glass with a parabolic cross-section are used to illuminate shop windows. They reflect the light perpendicularly down, so that the goods on display in the window are very brightly lit up' (C. Muchall, *Das A-B-C des Gas-Consumenten*, Wiesbaden, 1889, p. 23).

22. Bruno H. Jahn, *Reklame durch das Schaufenster* (Berlin, 1926), p. 130.

Night life. 'Glittering shops everywhere, splendid displays, cafés covered in gilt, and permanent lighting. . . . The shops put out so much light that one can read the paper as one strolls' (Julien Lemer, *Paris au gaz*, 1861).
(*Source*: *L'Electricité*, 1882)

literati, financiers. The whole thing resembles a drawing-room' — this is Emma von Niendorf's 1854 description of the Parisian Boulevard des Italiens late at night.[23] There is a simple psychological explanation for the fact that the street looks like an 'Interieur', to borrow Walter Benjamin's expression.[24] Any artificially lit area out of doors is experienced as an interior because it is marked off from the surrounding darkness as if by walls, which run along the edges of the lit up area. The same applies to the 'ceiling'. Common usage shows that we step *out* of the darkness *into* a circle of light — be it the small one of a camp fire

23. Emma von Niendorf, *Aus dem heutigen Paris* (Stuttgart, 1854), p. 171.
24. Walter Benjamin, *Charles Baudelaire. Ein Lyriker im Zeitalter des Hochkapitalismus* (Frankfurt, 1969), p. 37.

Vincent van Gogh: *Café at night*.
(Archiv für Kunst und Geschichte.)

or the larger one of a lighted boulevard. The 'side walls' of the
boulevard, as a 'room', were defined by the housefronts — shop
windows, restaurants and café terraces; its 'ceiling' was at the
limit of the commercial lighting, that is, at about first-floor level.

Before shop lighting created an 'interior' space out of doors,
however, it went through a transitional phase, developing in an
area that was bigger than the individual shop, but not yet as big
as the open boulevard: the glass-roofed arcade, gallery or pas-

Garden aspect of the Palais-Royal. 'It makes a splendid sight indeed —
tasteful Argand lamps illuminating the shops in the evening and at night,
luxury goods sparkling with a heightened brilliance, and bright *réverbères*
lighting up a packed, surging crowd in the arcades' (traveller's report, 1800).
(*Source*: A. Pugin and C. Heath, *Paris and Its Environs*, London, 1831.)

sage. This type of commercial space was most highly developed
in Paris. The Galérie Orléans in the Palais Royal, *the* centre of
Paris night life between 1790 and 1830, was the first of its kind.
'It makes a splendid sight indeed', reported a German traveller
in 1800 (i.e. before the introduction of gas lighting), 'tasteful
Argand lamps illuminating the shops in the evening and at
night, luxury goods sparkling with a heightened brilliance, and
bright *réverbères* lighting up a packed, surging crowd in the
arcades'.[25] Here is the same view under gaslight, described
thirty years later: 'A thousand lights are reflected in the surface
of polished mahogany and in the large mirror walls. . . . The
stranger dazzled by all this begins to think of the Palais Royal as
a bazaar'.[26] When the Palais Royal fell out of favour after 1830,
Paris's numerous arcades took over the role of the Galérie
Orléans in a process of decentralisation that was also an expan-

25. *Reise nach Paris im August und September 1789* (no place of publication, 1800), p. 180.
26. *Le livre des Cent-et-Un* (Paris, 1831), Vol. 1, pp. 19–21.

sion of night life. Contemporary descriptions of these new venues are couched in exactly the same terms as descriptions of the Galérie Orléans. People seem to have been fascinated by the interplay between the brilliance of the light and the wares on display, and the lively crowd. 'A labyrinth of iridescent passages, like rainbow bridges in an ocean of light. A totally magical world. Everything, or rather, much more than the imagination could devise.'[27]

There is a final step in this progression of light: the emergence of light from a roofed-in space into the open air. The following descriptions are of boulevards, but they could just as well be about arcades or the Galérie Orléans. 'Glittering shops everywhere, splendid displays, cafés covered in gilt, and permanent lighting. . . . The shops put out so much light that one can read the paper as one strolls.'[28] 'The gas-lamps sparkle and the suspended lamps glow, and in between there are the tobacconists' red lanterns and the chemists' blue-glass globes — transparent signs announce the marvels of the Paris night in large, fiery letters, and the crowd surges back and forth.'[29]

Impressions like these can be found in city guides and travel reports published between 1850 and 1870, with titles such as *Gas-Light and Day-Light*; *Paris au Gaz*; *Paris bei Sonnenschein und Lampenlicht*; and *New York by Gas*.[30] These two decades were the heyday of gas lighting. It had become firmly established in the cultural and psychological structure of Western European and American society. Earlier reservations and fears had disappeared, and its modern successor, electric light, had not yet arrived on the scene. Gaslight, like the railway, reigned supreme as a symbol of human and industrial progress.

All the same, gaslight still burned with an open flame. However functional, neutral and rational it seemed in comparison with earlier forms of lighting, it retained the lively, magical quality of an open flame. It was both a modern, expansive

---

27. Niendorf, *Aus dem heutigen Paris*, p. 169.
28. Lemer, *Paris au gaz*, p. 15.
29. Julius Rodenberg, *Paris bei Sonnenschein und Lampenlicht* (Leipzig, 1867), p. 45.
30. Detail on p. 142, n. 8, plus George G. Foster, *New York by Gas-Light* (New York, 1850). Lemer gives the following list of words relating to night life that were in vogue in Paris around 1860: *noctivague, noctilogue, noctiphague, noctiurge, physiologie de l'existence de nuit à Paris*.

Department store illumination (1883).
When the Magasins du Printemps in Paris installed electric lighting, the
technical journal *La Lumière électrique* reported: 'The impression made
by this gigantic glass palace is truly extraordinary. The powerful
electric light enlivens the whole quarter.'
(*Source: La Lumière électrique*, 1883.)

source of light that illuminated incomparably larger spaces than
any earlier form of lighting, and an 'old-fashioned' light still
bound to the flame. This combination was probably the source
of its appeal as a medium of night life in the capitals of Europe
between 1850 and 1870. Lighting up the night with gas stirred
people's feelings because it represented a triumph over the
natural order, achieved without the lifeless hardness of electric
light. Gaslight offered life, warmth and closeness. This was true
also of the relationship between light and the shop goods upon
which it fell. They were close to each other, indeed, they
permeated each other, and each enhanced the effect of the
other, to judge by descriptions of illuminated luxury shops.

Here, too, electric light injected an element of rigidity, coldness and distance. It burst open the 'ceiling' of the boulevard

'salon' by lifting it to roof level. From now on, commercial light shone down from this distant position, detached from the display windows, in its own, independent sphere. In 1928 Ernst May describes how this symphony of advertising lights in Times Square affected him: 'Here the eye does not read any writing, it cannot pick out any shapes, it is simply dazzled by a profusion of scintillating lights, by a plethora of elements of light that cancel out each other's effect.'[31]

31. Quoted from W. Lotz (ed.), *Licht und Beleuchtung* (Berlin, 1928), p. 44.

The Drawing-room

> Il faut donc avoir soin, à l'aide de rideaux, de
> stores, pendent la journée, le soir à l'aide
> d'abat-jours, d'écrans, etc., non seulement de
> modérer l'éclat du jour ou des lampes, mais
> de concentrer la lumière sur certains points,
> et de la ménager, de la sacrificer sur d'autres.
>
> (Henry Havard, *L'art dans la maison* 1884)*

In *The Philosophy of Furniture* Edgar Allan Poe remarks that gaslight is 'totally inadmissable within doors. Its harsh and unsteady light offends'.[1] This is the verdict of a hypersensitive aesthete, but it was also the general opinion of gaslight in the nineteenth century. In this view, gaslight was out of place in domestic rooms used for relaxing and entertaining. Interior decorating manuals, which were very popular at the end of the nineteenth century, advised people along the same lines. An 1889 French handbook says that gaslight 'is inadmissable in the dining-room or in any other recreational room'.[2] An English publication of 1878 goes into greater detail:

Few have felt the overpowering and sickening influence of a room liberally lighted by gas, and closely shut up, as frequently rooms are, at the time when gas is most required. It is equally injurious to decorations, be they pictures, papers, ceilings, or hangings; quickly making them dingy and dirty. The light given is intense but hard; and concentrated, as it usually is, in the middle of the room, is equally unpleasing from its potency when near, or its inefficiency when far off. For the reader, writer, embroiderer, or artist at ease, it is at once irritating and ineffective. Many plans have been tried to soften and manage the refractory brilliancy, but for a carefully and thoughtfully decorated drawing-room they are unavailable; ground

---

*(One must see to it that bright daylight or lamplight is not only softened, but also concentrated on particular spots and kept away from others — in short, that it is properly distributed. Curtains and blinds do this job during the day, lampshades of various sorts at night.)

1. E.A. Poe, *The Works*, ed. E.C. Stedman and G.E. Woodberry (Freeport, 1971 — reprint of the 1895 edn), Vol. 9, p. 217.

2. Emile Cardon, *L'Art au foyer domestique* (Paris, 1884), p. 69.

glass globes are ugly in shape and poor in colour, by day or by night.[3]

As far as we can tell from the surviving literature, gaslight really was excluded from the centre of the bourgeois home, the drawing-room. J.O.N. Rutter was a leading English gas engineer between 1830 and 1850 and an enthusiastic supporter of gaslight in the bourgeois home. In 1835 he listed the spaces in the home most suitable for it: 'Nurseries, bedrooms and libraries, dining-rooms, studies, servants' rooms and stables, cellars, taverns, warehouses and public buildings.'[4] The drawing-room, living room or parlour is missing.[5] Ten years later, Rutter could point out with satisfaction that gaslight had penetrated inside the house. But again, the drawing-room is missing from his list:

> For a long period after the manufacture of gas had been introduced into all the principal towns in the kingdom, it was considered as applicable only to the lighting of streets, shops, warehouses, factories, and public buildings. Its employment in the entrance-hall or stair-case of a well-furnished house was deemed a bold experiment; and when it advanced still further into the interior, and occupied the passages and domestic offices, many old-fashioned people shook their heads, looked grave, and predicted terrible consequences. These fears and forebodings have passed away; or, if in some dark corner a few of them still exist, along with a horror of rail-roads, steam-boats, and electric telelgraphs, they are exceptions to the feelings of confidence and satisfaction which so generally prevail wherever gas-light has had a fair trial.

3. Mrs Orrinsmith, *The Drawing Room, Its Decoration and Furniture*, in the series 'Art at Home' (London, 1878), pp. 111–12.

4. J.O.N. Rutter, *Das Ganze der Gasbeleuchtung, nach ihrem jetzigen Standpunkte* (Quedlinburg and Leipzig, 1835), p. 430.

5. The main room of the bourgeois home is sometimes called the drawing-room, sometimes the parlour or living-room. This seeming inconsistency reflects the indeterminacy of contemporary usage. Until well into the nineteenth century, the room that was reserved for celebrations and social gatherings was known as the drawing-room or parlour — a bourgeois imitation of the aristocratic salon. The family itself did not use this room. It lay like a foreign body, a lifeless centre in the bourgeois home until, in the second half of the nineteenth century, it gradually opened up to family life and evolved into the modern living-room. Drawing-room, parlour and living-room have a common root in the room where the family originally gathered around the fire. 'The function of this room is best described by reference to the stove that is its inalienable feature — it is not a room without a stove' (Konrad Bedal, *Historische Hausforschung*, Münster, 1978, p. 125). Stove, hearth, fire, light — the room that accommodated them in this order became the centre of the house.

Light in the drawing-room. For a long time, gaslight was 'almost completely excluded from living premises . . . and tolerated at most in corridors and kitchens' (Schilling, *Handbuch der Steinkohlengas-Beleuchtung*, 1866). By the end of the nineteenth century, it had penetrated to the centre of the house as well, as witnessed by the gas connections we can still see in old houses. In these two drawing-rooms, the light of candles, oil and paraffin lamps still reigns supreme (even in the chandelier) — it was obviously felt to be more refined.

(1) Anton von Werner, *Taufe im meinem Haus* (A Christening in My House), 1879, Bundespost Museum, Frankfurt. (2) Plate from Jules Janin, *The American in Paris*, 1844.)

Gazing into the flame.
(Detail from George de la Tour, *Sainte Madeleline*; see detail on p. 5.)

A remarkable circumstance connected with the progress of gas-lighting is that, of the many thousands of persons who have availed themselves of gas, never doubting that it was indispensable in their business transactions, so small a proportion, until very recently, should have thought it equally necessary to the comfort and convenience of their families.[6]

The fact that gaslight 'was still almost completely excluded from living premises . . . and tolerated at most in corridors and kitchens', as the second edition (1866) of Schilling's *Handbuch der Steinkohlengas-Beleuchtung* says,[7] cannot be explained by its novelty. Even as a technically perfected and firmly established part of European material culture, it remained banished to the periphery of the bourgeois home. 'If gaslight is limited to en-

---

6. Quoted from Dean Chandler and A. Douglas Lacey, *The Rise of the Gas Industry in Britain* (London, 1949), p. 76.

7. N.H. Schilling, *Handbuch für Steinkohlengas-Beleuchtung*, 2nd edn (Munich, 1866), p. 105.

trance halls, waiting-rooms, kitchens and public lighting, its principal disadvantages are not apparent, and its advantages can emerge unhampered.'[8] On closer inspection, the arguments advanced against admitting gaslight into the drawing-room do not hold water. The danger of poisoning or explosion, for instance,[9] was not diminished by cutting gas pipes short at the living-room door once the house and been connected to the mains. The argument that gaslight used up the air and that its combustion residues damaged the interior decoration of rooms,[10] was equally unfounded; candles and oil lamps used up oxygen too, and left behind even more combustion residues. These side effects were more noticeable with gaslight only because the flame was so much bigger. And finally, dazzling brightness was not a quality exclusive to gas either. The paraffin that had replaced oil since about 1800 provided light of roughly the same intensity.

The paraffin lamp, incidentally, is an excellent test case for the ✓ nineteenth-century psychology of lighting. The drawing-rooms and living-rooms that shut gaslight out welcomed the paraffin lamp in with no resistance. In the second half of the nineteenth century the paraffin lamp became 'living-room lighting *par excellence*'.[11] Its success is surprising, as technologically it was a step backwards from gaslight. (The paraffin lamp was merely an Argand lamp that had been adapted to use refined mineral oil instead of organic oil.) The preference for this type of lamp, which needed elaborate tending (the glass cylinder had to be cleaned, the wick trimmed and sometimes changed, the oil reservoir filled, etc.), over gaslight,which required no effort and was equally bright, is curious.

It seems to have been a reaction to the industrialisation of

8. Bouchardat, 'La Lumière et son action sur Oeil', *Revue scientifique*, 18 August 1879, p. 147.

9. See the 'Night Life' section in this book (pp. 135f.). Schilling, *Handbuch für Steinkohlengas-Beleuchtung*, 2nd edn (1866), p. 105, wrote: 'Its explosiveness and inflammability still prevent some people from installing it [gas lighting].'

10. *Journal of Science* (1820): 'The suffocating smell, and the property which it has of tarnishing everything metallic, exclude its use from dwelling-houses, on account of the injury it would do to our health, our furniture, books, pictures, plate, paint, etc... These effects render coal gas unpleasant in our sitting rooms, and have nearly confined its use to open shops and street lamps' (quoted from Matthews, *Historical Sketch*, p. 108).

11. L. Galine, *Traité général d' éclairage* (Paris, 1894), p. 408.

lighting. By keeping their independent lights, people symbolically distanced themselves from a centralised supply. The traditional oil-lamp or candle in a living-room expressed both a reluctance to be connected to the gas mains and the need for a light that fed on some visible fuel. This was obviously the point of the claim with which the French handbook quoted above followed up its verdict on gaslight: 'Lamp oil and candles are the only sources of light we can use in a room in which we want to feel comfortable with our families.'[12] What Bachelard has to say about the significance of the oil in a lamp reads like a commentary on this: 'A good lamp, a good wick, good oil — these are the prerequisites for a light that warms the heart. Anyone who values a beautiful flame must also value good oil. . . . For Novalis, oil is nothing less than the essence of the flame; beautiful, yellow oil is like condensed light that wants to expand. With a small flame, we free the light trapped in this material form.'[13] Visibly devouring its fuel, the candle or oil-lamp was, in fact, a miniature fire. Looking at it evoked the same dreamy thoughts as looking at the fire in an open fireplace, described so vividly by Bachelard. And indeed, the open light succeeded to the place that had been occupied by the ancient hearth fire. Until the end of the nineteenth century, the peasant household would gather around the light in the living-room every evening when the day's work was done. The light was mostly placed directly next to the stove or on the table — both positions relate to the original hearth.[14] The fire that had disappeared into the stove underwent a sublimated resurrection in the open light, a stand-in for the fire that the eye obviously still needed. 'Um des Lichts gesell'ge Flamme/Sammeln sich die Hausbewohner' (Around the light's convivial flame/the household gathers), wrote Schiller in *Die Glocke*. The scene is described in folklore as well as poetry: 'Here the household gathers around the stove and the light after the evening meal. What envelops everyone and remains so firmly fixed in the villager's memory is the complexity of the

12. Cardon, *L'Art au foyer domestique.*
13. Gaston Bachelard, *La Flamme d'une chandelle* (Paris, 1961), pp. 93–4.
14. The hearth, originally in the middle of a one-roomed house, was eventually moved over to a wall. Its place was taken by the table, the focus of domestic life, especially meals (Herbert Freudenthal, *Das Feuer im deutschen Glauben und Brauch*, Berlin and Leipzig, 1931, p. 54). The lamp placed on or over the table can therefore be seen as a relic of the original hearth fire.

Light and the communal household. 'Here the household gathers around the
stove and the light after the evening meal. What envelops everyone and
remains so firmly fixed in the villager's memory is the complexity of the
"living room in the evening". It includes the comfort and cosiness of the
warm, dimly lit room, and the feeling of togetherness linking those sitting
crowded around the light and the stove' (J. Feige).
(*above*) Ludwig Richter (Science Museum, London)

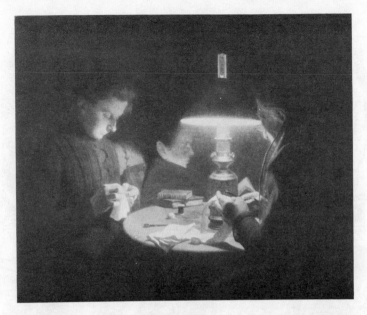

Henry Marius Camilles Bouvet, *Familie beim Lampenschein* (Family by
Lamplight), 1902
(Archiv für Kunst und Geschichte, Berlin)

Adolf von Menzel, *Abendgesellschaft bei Justizrat Maercker* (Soirée at
Justizrat Maercker's)
(Archiv für Kunst und Geschichte, Berlin)

Sigmund Freudeberg, *Der Winterabend* (A Winter's Evening), 1774
(Archiv für Kunst und Geschichte)

"living-room in the evening". It includes the comfort and cosiness of the warm, dimly lit room, and the feeling of togetherness linking those sitting crowded around the light and the stove.'[15]

Some autobiographical scenes of communal evening life confirm that the light played a central part. 'At supper time', reads the autobiography of one peasant, 'a small tin oil-lamp was placed on an upturned pot in the middle of the table. Gradually, all the members of the household would quietly gather around it.'[16] The situation was similar in the bourgeois (or rather, petty bourgeois) home. 'In the evening, our parents and the older children would sit around the round table in the living-room. Two lamps burned brightly in the middle of the room. Mother worked as usual, but the rest of us would read.'[17] 'The evenings, when the lamp was burning above the round table and the family was gathered around it, chatting, reading or working, were always a special time'.[18] An open light was also like a miniature fire in that it needed constant attention, most obviously in the process of trimming the wick. Around 1800, the wick of an average candle was trimmed about forty-five times.[19] 'I can still see father, sitting at the table and listening', we read in another autobiographical account, 'staring into the oil-lamp with a fixed gaze, and poking at the wick with the lamp trimmer on a chain in a preoccupied way.'[20]

Seeing the hearth fire as the archetype of the living-room light not only explains the persistence of an open light but also says a great deal about nineteenth- century perceptions of light. The reddish glow produced by a wood fire and other organic fuels

15. Johannes Feige, *Der alte Feierabend*, Arbeiten zur Entwicklungspsychologie, Vol. 17 (Munich, 1936), p. 15. In his story 'Das kalte Herz', Wilhelm Hauff depicts the following domestic scene: 'After the evening meal, the woman of the house and her daughters took their spindles and sat down around the large fire brand that the youngsters fed with the finest fir resin. Grandfather, the guest and the landlord smoked and watched the women, while the young men were busy carving wooden spoons and forks' (*Sämtliche Werke*, Munich, n.d. [1970], Vol. 2, p. 222).

16. Josef Meder, *Leben und Meinungen eines alten Bauernjungen* (Vienna and Leipzig, 1918), quoted from Feige, *Der alte Feierabend*, p. 15.

17. Paul Hertz, *Unser Elternhaus* (1913), quoted from ibid., p. 80.

18. Lily Braun, *Im Schatten der Titanen* (1910), quoted from ibid., p. 85.

19. *Monthly Magazine* (1805), quoted from Peckston, *Theory and Practice of Gas-Lighting*, p. 38.

20. Polack, *Brosamen*, quoted from Feige, *Der alte Feierabend*, p. 19.

was regarded as the normal and natural type of light. Until the end of the eighteenth century all lighting, whether in a work-shop, a drawing-room or the hall of mirrors at Versailles, was of this basic gentle type. The only factors that varied were the number of lights and the quality of the fuel. Even the largest collection of candles could not really be dazzling, as it consisted only of individual weak lights. The thousands of candles used in a festive illumination at Versailles never created an unstructured mass of light; they produced a gentle aura that drew body and life from all the individual flames. Characteristic of this old culture of lighting was that its effect was direct, achieved through the impact of the flame itself.

The flame lost this quality in the Argand lamp, which trans-formed the old flame, with its almost poetic qualities, into a harsh core of light. To look at it directly was not merely unpleas-ant, it was impossible. 'A rear view of the naked flame of an Argand lamp is quite insupportable, as is well known', the chemist and inventor Count Rumford (1753–1814) remarked in about 1800.[21] He also coined some beauty advice: women who cared what they looked like should not show themselves in the pitiless beams of an Argand lamp.[22] Rumford was the first person to work out systematically how to deal with this new type of light — that is, by shading it:

> The only way in which the flames of lamps and candles can be masked, without occasioning a great loss of light, is to cover them with screens composed of such substances as disperse the light without destroying it. Ground glass, thin white silk stuffs, such as gauze and crape, fine white paper, horn, and various other sub-stances, may be used for that purpose, and have been used very often.[23]

As Rumford informs us, this practice, probably inspired by Japanese lanterns, was already widespread by the beginning of the nineteenth century.[24] These new shades had nothing in

---

21. Benjamin Count Rumford, *The Complete Works* (Boston, n.d.), Vol. 4, p. 106.
22. Ibid., p. 134.
23. Ibid., p. 106.
24. 'This contrivance has been in use several years, in most parts of Europe, for moderat-ing the too powerful brightness of Argand's beautiful lamp' (ibid., p. 106).

common with existing shades. The only lamps that were shaded at that time were study lamps, which had been used since the seventeenth century. Their shades were not designed to disperse and mute the light; on the contrary, they concentrated the light of a candle on a book or some other article.

The new type of lampshade was, in fact, the result of applying to lighting the same ancient principle that governed the stove. As the open fire had disappeared into the stove, which radiated its 'abstract' quality in the form of warmth, so the lampshade filtered an 'abstract' light out of the flame. (The fact that lighting took so long to assimilate the old techniques of the fire says something about the marginal position of lighting in eighteenth-century European culture. After all, the glass cylinder of the Argand lamp was nothing but a 'chimney'.)

Lampshades could be seen as a negative development because they hid the flame; but they could equally well be considered a positive transformation of the light, in which a glowing shade replaced the light of the flame. Rumford wrote:

> The rays of light will be so dispersed in passing through it [the spherical shade] that from each visible point of its external surface rays will be sent off in all directions which will render the surface of the globe *luminous*. The flame of the candle will no longer be seen through it, but surrounding bodies will not be less illuminated on that account. *The globe will be the only luminous body which will be visible.* [second emphasis added][25]

Contemporary descriptions emphasised the evenness of the light cast by shaded lamps. Rumford described it as 'mild and uniformly distributed', and more or less the same terms recur in most other accounts. In the 1817 issue of *Annalen der Physik*, for example, it is called 'steadier, milder and more constant than candle light'.[26] Diffusing the flame's direct light, the shade also changed how things looked by altering the shadows they cast. 'Because the contours of the actual flame become blurred', we read in a book on the art of illuminating buildings, rooms and streets, published in 1835, 'all the rays of light emanate from the surface of the bell, which thus itself seems to glow. For this

25. Ibid., p. 109.
26. *Annalen der Physik* (1817), p. 400.

reason as well as because the rays that it sends out cross over each other in all directions, objects in its vicinity can only cast short, imperceptible shadows.'[27]

At about the same time, a different sort of natural light was also wanted in rooms. Windows, which until about 1800 had been as 'naked' as the candle flame itself, were 'clothed' in the early nineteenth century. At first, just the top of the window was draped very simply in order to reduce the glare from the brightest light. Soon, however, the whole surface of the window was covered by curtains. What the shade of transparent, white material did for the lamp, the muslin curtain did for the window. The objective was the same: to dampen and diffuse light that was regarded as too intense, hard and aggressive. Cornelius Gurlitt, a writer on art who described the introduction of curtains from the perspective of 1888 (certainly projecting the attitudes of his own times), suggested reasons for this sudden aversion to overly bright light. The equation he drew, quite ✓ naïvely, between light and exposure to public view gives us an important clue to nineteenth-century perceptions of light. According to Gurlitt, the aim of introducing curtains at the beginning of the nineteenth century was 'to close the room to unknown eyes from outside and to the cold sobriety of daylight, without destroying one's enjoyment of the light. The idea arose of hanging a light, transparent material over the window. The deeper shadows in its broad folds would soften the window's severe architectural lines, without cutting out the light completely. White material was chosen because at that time white was considered the height of good taste'.[28] Transparent white materials such as muslin and gauze were used not only to drape lamps and windows in the early nineteenth century but also for clothing. Women's fashions under the Empire developed a real craze for muslin. Diaphanous clothes let the flesh shimmer through just as curtains let the window-frame shine through, but wearing such garments frequently resulted in epidemics of colds, often called 'muslin sickness' at the time.[29] Probably the strangest outgrowth of the fashion for muslin was the 'muslin

27. E. Peclet, *Die Kunst der Gebäude-, Zimmer- und Straßenbeleuchtung durch Oel, Talg, Wachs und Gas* (Weimar, 1853), p. 150.
28. Cornelius Gurlitt, *Im Bürgerhaus* (Dresden, 1888), p. 166.
29. Max von Boehn, *Modes and Manners of the 19th Century*, Vol. 1, p. 124.

The curtain. 'The aim was to close the room to unknown eyes from outside and to the cold sobriety of daylight, without destroying one's enjoyment of the light. The idea arose of hanging a light, transparent material over the window . . . which would soften the window's severe architectural lines, without cutting out the light completely' (Cornelius Gurlitt).
(*above*) Adolph von Menzel, *Das Balkonzimmer* (Room with Balcony), 1845 (Archiv für Kunst und Geschichte, Berlin)

Georg Friedrich Kersting, *Vor dem Spiegel* (In Front of the Mirror)
(Archiv für Kunst und Geschichte)

cabinet' that Schinkel built for the Charlottenburg Palace in
Berlin in 1829, using 380 ells of material.[30]

The preference for diffuse, white light and filmy, white materials can, of course, be explained by the dominant neo-classical
taste in colours, which placed a high value on the non-colour
white. For our purposes, however, this general background is
less informative than the painting of the period, especially the
works of C.D. Friedrich, Gainsborough and Runge. Their treatment of light is related to the type of light created by using
lampshades and curtains. Wolfgang Schöne, who points out
that eighteenth-century painters had already aspired to achieve
the effect of diffused light, describes the phenomenon as follows: 'The dualism of light and darkness is to a large extent
cancelled: shadows lose substance, and light gains in
strength.'[31] At that period, painters preferred to depict light 'as
veiled sunlight'.[32] According to Schöne, light was completely
liberated in the first open-air art, the landscape painting of the
early nineteenth century. It was dominated by 'a free light that,
by its very nature, permeates the entire visible world of the
painting. Thus the viewer perceives its source as *infinitely
distant*. . . . By contrast to this, every painting of the fifteenth to
eighteenth centuries resembles a bowl that is of varying size but
always closed and filled with a *close* light, right to its edges but
not beyond' (emphases added).[33]

This is not to suggest that the treatment of light in painting
directly influenced the sort of light that people tried to create
with lampshades and curtains, or vice versa. But it is clear that

30. Meier-Oberist, *Kulturgeschichte des Wohnens im abendländischen Raum* (Hamburg, 1956),
p. 252.

31. Wolfgang Schöne, *Über das Licht in der Malerei*, 4th edn (Berlin, 1977), p. 161.

32. Ibid., p. 162.

33. Ibid., p. 194. An early description of this new quality of nineteenth-century painting
can be found in a small book by the English painter Henry Richter, *Day-Light: A Recent
Discovery in the Art of Painting* (London, 1817), which Schöne mentions. It consists of an
imaginary conversation between a contemporary art lover and the Old Masters of
seventeenth-century Dutch painting. The young man, speaking for the author, asks the
Spirits of these Great Men: 'But, pray, was there no *clear Sky* in your days? and did not *the
broad blue light of the atmosphere* shine then as it does now? It is *this* which I mean by the term
Day-light, as distinguished from *the direct light of the Sun*. And *this light from the Sky*
should fall perpendicularly upon the *tops* of all objects, whether the Sun shine upon them or
not' (pp. 2–3, original emphases).

'CHRISTIANIA' OR ARGAND BURNER

The gas flame disguised.
The naked core of light is considered to be ugly. It
disappears behind shades made of cloth or opaque,
painted or ground glass, which give an aesthetically
filtered light.

the same new preference for bright, diffused light was expressed in both painting and domestic lighting tastes. The light
in early nineteenth-century paintings seemed as *distant* as that
cast by lampshades. This distancing from a *close* light, set off
these new forms from earlier painting and earlier lighting techniques.

A flame that no longer cast light directly but merely served to
make a transparent white ball glow from inside had been reduced to a machine for generating light. It produced light as a
'raw material' that had to be 'refined' by the lampshade before it
could be admitted into the drawing-room. In addition, the body
of the lamp itself was now disguised. The Argand lamp was, in
fact, a small machine for manufacturing light. It lacked the slim
lines and simple elegance of the candle, and this was noticed all
the more for the fact that traditionally the oil-lamp had been
used to illuminate workshops and the homes of poor people.
Until the end of the eighteenth century only candles had been
used in the houses of the upper classes. This monopoly was
broken by the Argand lamp.[34] Its complicated construction,
however, made it aesthetically displeasing, and so covering up
the working parts was an obvious thing to do. As Rumford
points out, 'all that is ugly and disgusting in a lamp may be
concealed'.[35] The lamps that he built 'were so covered by large
screens of white gauze, in the form of flat dome or truncated
cone, as to conceal the lamps entirely from the view'.[36] The lamp
shade was something like the body of a carriage, that concealed
the necessary, but 'ugly', machinery beneath. The introduction
of the paraffin lamp further encouraged the division of the lamp
into a technical and a decorative part. In its 1897 issue, the
German journal *Zeitschrift für Beleuchtungswesen* writes:

> Only the foot of the lamp, the oil reservoir and, at most, the bell, are
> the province of the artist. All the rest, — the mechanical parts such as
> the burner and the cylinder — is factory-produced. This dualism
> means that the lamp is a hybrid. Half of it is created by the living

34. E. Peclet, *Traité de l'éclairage* (Paris, 1827), Vol. 1, p. 1.
35. Rumford, *The Complete Works*, Vol. 4, p. 110.
36. Ibid.

Gaslights (1814). 'What a marvellous invention is gas lighting! What means it gives us for enriching . . . our festivities! Nevertheless, people try to disguise the nozzles of gas pipes in their drawing rooms so that they look like candles or oil-lamps' (Gottfried Semper).
(*Source*: Accum, *A Practical Treatise on Gas-Light*.)

hands of artists and reflects their personalities . . . while something of the deathly chill and hardness typical of machine-made products adheres to the other half. The soul of a work of art is chained to the dead body of a machine. For this reason, the lamp — half machine and half work of art — will never achieve a form as satisfying as an ornamental vase, for instance. The protruding element of the cylinder, or the wick mechanism will always destroy the pure aesthetic pleasure conferred by a work of art.[37]

Gaslight, as far as it was used in living spaces at all, presented a different decorating problem. It was not a complete lamp but, as Schilling puts it, merely 'a pipe, adorned to a greater or lesser

37. *Zeitschrift für Beleuchtungswesen*, no. 6 (1897), p. 55.

degree, and equipped with a tap'.[38] By imitating old styles in the decoration of this pipe or burner, manufacturers tried to bring the abstract industrial product into line with the tastes of consumers. (Elsewhere, Schilling speaks of the gas mains as 'connected on the one hand with the gasometer and on the other with the . . . lamps, thus linking producer and consumer',[39] an unsurpassed description of the industrial nature of gaslight.)

The desire to produce attractive gaslights ushered in the age of ornamental lamps. One of the first to criticise these attemps to dress up new technology in old styles was Gottfried Semper. 'What a marvellous invention is gas lighting', he exclaimed. 'What means it gives us for enriching . . . our festivities! Nevertheless, people try to disguise the nozzles of gas pipes in their drawing rooms so that they look like candles or oil-lamps.'[40] Almost fifty years later, Julius Lessing made the same complaint: 'The same old chandeliers, with a stem, branches and candles, are used. The fact that air is being burnt here, that these chandeliers are supplied by pipes, is hidden . . . and candles are retained — false, porcelain candles.'[41] As we know, dressing up the outside of industrial products in historical styles was a general trend in the nineteenth century. We can see it at work in the façades of railway stations as well as in lamps. Shades fulfilled a similar decorative function for the industrial 'raw material' light; by conferring shape upon it, they restored the form that it had lost through industrialisation.

During the course of the nineteenth century, the colour of lampshades gradually got darker. On the one hand this can be explained by a change in taste, a general preference for darker hues in painting, interior decoration and clothing. But there is also a much more direct explanation which, it is true, is also closely connected with changes in prevailing tastes. The darkening of lampshades is an obvious reaction to an increase in the intensity of artificially produced light. As lights got brighter, lampshades got darker.

This was a slow process. The shades of gaslights or paraffin

---

38. Schilling, *Handbuch für Steinkohlengas-Beleuchtung*, 2nd edn (1866), p. 379.
39. Ibid, p. 326.
40. Gottfried Semper, *Wissenschaft, Industrie und Kunst* (1851; reprinted Mainz 1966), p. 33.
41. Julius Lessing, 'Elektrische Beleuchtungskörper', *Westermanns Monatshefte*, October 1894, p. 100.

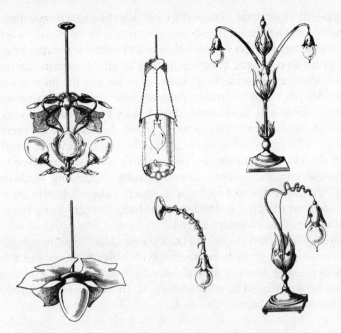

Electric lights (1887). 'The light is enclosed not in a boring cylinder or
clumsy dome, but in a glass casing that can be of almost any shape
desired. . . . The shape of the light bulb, following the curves of the
spirally rolled filament, practically calls out to be surrounded by a
flower, where it represents the pistil. Or it could be given the colour
and shape of a piece of fruit. The plant world offers endlessly new and
charming possibilities. The presentation of the bulb as a flower or a
fruit tends to result in the plant motif being continued throughout the
whole lamp' (*Zeitschrift für Beleuchtungswesen*, 1897)
(*Source: La Lumière électrique*, 1887.)

lamps generally retained the white used for Argand lampshades, but alleviated its monotony by adding some sort of
ornamentation. Depending on what material the shade was
made of, decorations were painted or sewn onto it, or cut or
ground into it. It was important that they did not absorb too
much light, for although gas and paraffin lamps were brighter
than Argand lamps, they were not yet powerful enough to allow
really light-absorbing shades to be used. The shade was still
essentially intended to diffuse the intense core of the flame into

a type of light that was easier on the eyes, without losing valuable quantities of it.[42]

Electric light called for completely different treatment, not so much because it was brighter (the light of the carbon-filament lamp was only about as bright as that of the gas flame, and light intensity did not increase dramatically until the tungsten-filament bulb was developed), but mainly because it was incandescent light, which possessed a hard, disembodied, abstract quality. The open flame of gaslight linked it, however distantly, with the old unity of fire and light, but no reminiscence of this lingered with incandescent electric light. According to Bachelard, the incandescent bulb 'will never allow us to dream the dreams that the light of the living oil-lamp conjured up. We live in the age of administered light.'[43]

The art historian Wilhelm Hausenstein describes the sobering effect of electric light as compared with older forms of light. He experienced it himself when, during Second World War air raids, he was forced to use candlelight. In a diary entry dated 16 September 1944 he wrote:

> Of late the electric light often fails. Then we depend on the few candles that we have saved. Because we have reached the stage at which we experience everything positive twice or three times over, we have noticed that in the 'weaker' light of a candle, objects have a different, a much more marked profile — it gives them a quality of 'reality'. This is something that is lost in electric light: objects (seemingly) appear much more clearly, but in reality it *flattens* them. Electric light imparts too much brightness and thus things lose body, outline, substance — in short, their essence. In candlelight objects cast much more significant shadows, shadows that have the power actually to create forms. Candles give as much light as things need in order to be what they are — optimally, so to speak — and allows them to retain their poetic element.[44]

---

42. G.M.S. Blochmann, *Fünf Vorträge über Beleuchtung für Gasconsumenten* (Dresden, 1873), p. 36: 'In order to obtain the maximum amount of light while protecting the eye from the direct light of the flame, a large opening is made in the top of the glass shade. This allows as much light as possible to go up to the ceiling from where it is diffused by reflection.'

43. Bachelard, *La Flamme*, p. 90.

44. Wilhelm Hausenstein, *Licht unter dem Horizont, Tagebücher von 1942 bis 1946* (Munich, 1967), p. 273. (I am grateful to Carl-Friedrich Bauman from Essen for the reference to this passage.)

How did the interiors of bourgeois homes, and their occupants, react to this prosaic, disembodied light at the end of the nineteenth century? To start with, the focal point of the home, the place where the family gathered, disappeared along with candles and the paraffin lamp. The light bulb lacked the flame's magical power of attraction. Soon, however, an electrical substitute developed. The gramophone and later the radio provided a new centre around which the family would gather in the evenings, as they had once sat around the fire of the light.[45] The situation was a little uncanny, however, with the family concentrating on a purely acoustic device, the loudspeaker, as though there were something to see. The introduction of television again satisfied this instinctive need to watch something, a drive produced by thousands of years of contemplating the hearth fire.

Electric light not only dissolved the centre around which the family gathered; it also altered the whole appearance of the rooms that it lit up, or rather, inundated with light. To start with, the colours used to decorate rooms which had been toned to fit in with existing levels of light, looked different, as an English manual of *Practical House Decoration* (1886) points out:

> Where he [the owner of an apartment] would have placed delicate or pronounced *warm* tints as a counterfoil to the rays from an Edison or a Brush incandescent lamp, he finds that he has retained the cold tones, rendered still more sterile by its uncompromisingly searching brilliancy, and the pleasing satisfaction of knowing that he has put the right tint in the right place is denied him forthwith.[46]

In the long run the only way around such an unpleasant effect was to adjust the colours used in interior decorating to the qualities of electric light. In fact, Henry Havard saw electric light as the main factor in developing the particular taste in colours that was fashionable at his time: 'This is the origin of the preference for pale wall papers, colourless materials and old wall hangings that is so characteristic of our age. Muted colours are more compatible with the lively lighting in our homes than

---

45. 'The radio is a modern substitute for the hearth-side' (Hadley Cantril and Gordon W. Allport, *The Psychology of the Radio* (New York and London, 1935), p. 15.

46. James William Facey, *Practical House Decoration* (London, 1886), p. 25.

are the more vigorous colours of new materials.'[47]

To return to the lampshade, the question is: how was it transformed by electric light, or how did it help to 'refine' the new medium? Around 1900, when the tungsten-filament light bulb (as opposed to the carbon-filament lamp) made available an efficient and cheap form of electric light that illuminated the furthest corners of every room evenly and without shadows, a totally new way of shading light was needed. Lighting technology had changed, as witnessed, for example, by the societies and journals that were founded after 1900. They were mainly interested in using the levels of light that had already been achieved, rather than in increasing them further, in 'the *use*, in contradiction to the *production* of light', as it was put in 1906, in the American Illuminating Engineering Society's inaugural address.[48] The reasons for this change were explained as follows.

> Though much attention has recently been given to the subject of globes, shades and reflectors, the fact still remains that unshaded or inadequately shaded lamps are the rule rather than the exception. In considering the present status of the science and art of illumination, there is perhaps no question that is in need of more immediate attention than this one. The practice of placing lights of excessive intrinsic brightness within the ordinary field of vision is so common as to cause grave apprehension among those who have studied the question from a physiological point of view, that our eyesight is suffering permanent injury. . . . Much of the trouble due to this cause would be removed if the light sources were screened or concealed, and the illuminating power from them derived from reflected rather than from direct rays. Happily the tendency of modern illumination is in this direction.[49]

While the white shades of Argand burners and paraffin lamps had still cast direct though diffused light, a whole new culture of lighting now developed, based on indirect, reflected and focused light. Traditionally the illuminated space had been structured by the range of the light cast by individual lamps or

47. Henry Havard, *Le Décoration* (Paris, n.d.), p. 141.
48. *Illuminating Engineering Society, Transactions*, Vol. 1, p. 4.
49. Ibid., pp. 5–6.

candles, now that the whole room was evenly lit up, it became necessary to create a structure artificially. The lampshade's new job was to carve a specific atmosphere out of the homogenous raw material of light. After 1900 an almost scientifically precise art of illumination developed. It divided up what had so far been a *total light* into various basic forms: direct and indirect, diffused and focused, localised and generalised. Well-balanced living-room lighting was composed of these various elements, as the following account suggests:

> A safe rule is that there should be enough diffused light, from illuminated walls and ceiling, so that all parts of the room can be clearly seen. To this add directed light at the points of interest — the work table, piano, or book page. The amount of this directed light will vary greatly according to the kind of room. In the dining-room a very considerable concentration of light on the table is permissible and desirable. In the small living-room or library, rather strong local lighting makes for cosiness.[50]

Before, we distinguished between 'close' (i.e. traditional) and 'distant' (i.e. modern) light. The lampshade worked a transformation: distant, amorphous electric light was turned into close, cosy light. This is almost the direct opposite of how the Argand lampshade functioned: it turned 'close' light into 'distant' light by hiding the flame. Different materials and colours were needed to cope with electric light; lampshades were no longer white but were made of darker, light-absorbing colours. Louis Bell, author of the first book on the art of illumination (1902), claimed: 'For artistic reasons it is sometimes desirable to reduce the illumination to a deep mellow glow quite irrespective of economy, and in such cases shades may be made ornamental to any degree and of any density required.'[51] Because bright light was no longer as expensive as it had been in the age of the carbon filament lamp, it could be filtered almost at will to produce warmer, darker shades. 'Unusually fine globes of new glass resembling old alabaster have recently made their appearance in the market', says an architectural journal of 1913,

50. W.C. Posey, *Hygiene of the Eye* (Philadelphia and London, 1918), pp. 112–13.
51. Louis Bell, *The Art of Illumination* (New York, 1902), pp. 164–5.

some of them having a rich soft brown tone which, when lighted produces a light that is commonly mellow and agreeable and being fairly dense in nature acts as a good reflector, giving the indirect effect. The brown tone while warm and of pleasing colour, it will be noted, is neutral as regards colour harmony and can be used with any other colour in a room's decoration.[52]

This type of lighting reached its peak in the 1890s, with the development of Tiffany lampshades. The kaleidoscope of light they cast was reminiscent of that produced by Gothic church windows. Julius Lessing wrote in 1894: 'An infinite variety and mixture of colours is created in this way. The most attractive shades are developed, ranging from the softest tones to the most gorgeous ones.'[53] Tiffany lampshades derived their peculiar liveliness from both the colour and the calculated irregularities in the structure of the glass that they were made of, which compensated for the monotony of electric light. The 1898 issue of a German journal of lighting describes how this type of glass was produced:

Iridescent glass flux, shimmering in all the colours of the rainbow and creating the most delicate nuances, develops a wavy, irregular surface when the substance is compressed before it cools. As it possesses some darker and some lighter patches, its permeability to light varies. Different effects are achieved by knocking pieces out of larger blocks of glass. The irregular fractures generate a varied play of light.[54]

Tiffany glass was used for windows as well as lampshades. Thus the parallels between the lamp and the window that were already visible in the early-nineteenth-century use of muslin to regulate natural and artificial light continued at the end of the century. 'Dressing up' lamps and windows in lightweight, white materials was no longer enough. Natural daylight that fell into the room through the window suddenly seemed hard, aggressive, and pitilessly white, rather like 'raw' electric light. The window itself, as the opening through which this incursion

52. *Architectural Record* (New York), vol. 33 (1913), p. 154.
53. Lessing, 'Elektrische Beleuchtungskörper', p. 103.
54. *Zeitschrift für Beleuchtungswesen*, no. 1 (1898), p. 9.

took place, was perceived as threatening. It was seen as a
yawning hole, 'a large, single, sharply delimited mass of light',
as the art writer Jacob von Falke says in 1882. 'Technically it is a
triumph, but we are so free as to make aesthetic demands as
well. . . . The dazzling mass of light hurts our eyes; we have the
feeling . . . that an empty surface is staring at us, like a blank
space in a painting.'[55] For the English author, Mrs Orrinsmith,
windows are 'usually so ugly that there is nothing pleasant
about them to look at. . . . No one could possibly detect properties of beauty in large sheets of glass'.[56]

Something was needed to fill in this faceless blank, to decorate it as the gas burner and the gas flame had been decorated.
Inspired by William Morris, a renaissance of medieval glass
painting began in about 1870, eventually culminating in the
production of Tiffany glass. The formless, flat surface of glass
was divided up into a number of small bull's eye panes, which
gave the light entering the window a new structure. According
to Falke, 'the purpose of window painting is to break up the
dazzling, formless mass of light from the window, and to
incorporate it as an artistic element into the decoration of the
rest of the room'.[57] The light that falls into the room through a
painted window 'replaces the empty space with a picture; it [the
glass painting] confers poetry on the room, consecrates it, gives
it life and warmth, thus removing it from the prosaic, the
everyday; attractive in itself, in harmony with its surroundings,
it covers the opulence of the room with the radiance of trans-
figuration'.[58] Havard emphasised the capacity of a painted window to separate an interior space from a desolate outdoors. He
saw the window as a coloured filter that held grey reality at bay:
'Its lively and harmoniously blended colours can brighten a dull,
grey day.'[59] For Cornelius Gurlitt, similarly, a painted window
guaranteed a warm atmosphere inside the room as against the
outside world:

The whole room is dusky, hidden. We feel alone in it, be it with our

55. Jacob von Falke, *Die Kunst im Hause* (Vienna, 1882), p. 326.
56. Orrinsmith, *The Drawing Room*, pp. 64–5.
57. Falke, *Die Kunst im Hause*, p. 330.
58. Ibid., p. 328.
59. Henry Havard, *L'Art dans la maison. Grammaire de l'ammeublement* (Paris, 1884), p. 301.

thoughts or with our friends. What is happening outside is far away. We cannot even see the passing of the clouds through the greenish light. We are enveloped by a special light — artificial like that of the lamp, but one that does not brighten one part of the room while leaving the rest in darkness. Instead, its refracted tints dissolve the shadows and give the light a more gentle, milder radiance, and a thoroughly artistic colouring.[60]

Curtains were also used to regulate the amount of light coming in through the windows. While painted windows acted as a coloured filter, curtains reduced the undivided mass of light from outside into manageable portions. Havard wrote: 'The amount of daylight we allow into the room and the clair-obscure effects we want to achieve depend on the number, the quality and the thickness of the curtains.'[61] A curtain that could be used to control and shape the light in this way had to be made of different material from the curtains of the early nineteenth century, which had not affected light intensity. In fact, the parallel development of curtains and lamp shades continues, and both now get darker and thicker. As the light bulb disappeared behind dark coloured shades, only a weak glimmer of light still hinting at its presence, so windows were also deliberately veiled, often under several layers of curtains at once. The result was the oft-cited twilight atmosphere of the bourgeois interior. Hirth gives us an impression of what it was like, writing from the critical distance of a time when things were about to change:

Huge, gathered curtains with many folds of heavy, dark material prevent the best light from entering the room through the top parts of the window, the opening for light is reduced to a triangle whose tip barely reaches the top one third of the window, and this already meagre light is then additionally filtered by white, tulle curtains. Even in the most fashionable districts of our large cities, windows display this sort of light-deadening aspect from the outside, and the 'refined' people who sit bored behind these clouds of cotton think it is 'stylish' and 'smart'. One needs the eyes of a cat to see anything properly in rooms like these.[62]

60. Gurlitt, *Im Bürgerhaus*, p. 168.
61. Havard, *L'Art dans la maison*, p. 300.
62. Georg Hirth, *Das deutsche Zimmer der Gothik und Renaissance, des Barock-Rokoko- und Zopfstils* (Munich and Leipzig, 1899), pp. 162–3.

The desire to create muted, interior lighting that was clearly different from daylight — whether achieved by painted glass windows or dark curtains — was something new in bourgeois tastes in home décor. After all, in the sixteenth century, when these tastes began to develop, there was a great hunger for light. Falke wrote:

> The Renaissance had done away with the coloured, twilight atmosphere, the secretive gloom which had been created in houses by narrow, irregular windows, inadequate locks and coloured glass. Once locking glass windows no longer presented any difficulty and locks had become widely available, houses were literally opened up to the light, just as minds were opening to the light of the new century — its humanism, arts and sciences, and its freedom of conscience and thought. In crowded, city houses, walls facing on to the street were made up almost entirely of windows and nothing but windows, separated only by the walls and beams necessary to carry the weight of what was above.[63]

Until about 1800, no distinction was made in the bourgeois home between interior and exterior light. The same daylight prevailed indoors and out — a harmonious co-existence classically depicted in seventeenth-century Dutch painting. Meier-Oberist commented on the windows in these paintings: 'They light up the interiors of rooms, without breaching the integrity of the space, and one does not even notice the lack of curtains.'[64] This light was neither aggressive and threatening, nor intimate and cosy, as it became to nineteenth-century perceptions. Rather, it possessed the same 'natural' uniformity as the artificial lighting of the pre-industrial period.

The evolution of *homogeneous light* into two increasingly different species, *outside light* and *inside light* (or *distant* and *close* light), relates to the wider social process by which the public and the private were increasingly separated in bourgeois life. This process started in the eighteenth century and reached its climax in the nineteenth century with the Industrial Revolution. The anxiety with which everything private, and especially the family, was shut off from a public that was felt to be more and more

63. Falke, *Die Kunst im Hause*, pp. 163–4.
64. Meier-Oberist, *Kulturgeschichte des Wohnens*, p. 150.

unpleasant, is reflected in attempts to prevent light from the street from falling directly into rooms. 'To be beneficial in our living-rooms', said Mrs Orrinsmith about light and air, 'they must be, as it were, educated to accord with indoor life'.[65] If light could not be reduced to what Mrs Orrinsmith called 'discreet doses', it was regarded as a distasteful intruder, an incursion of the outside world that had to be carefully filtered out. 'We find it difficult to concentrate in a room that is brightly lit by outside light, and the thought of being exposed to unwanted glances from outside is also disturbing'[66] — outside light, that is light that shone into the room from the street, made people feel uncomfortable, as this comment made by Karl Rosner in 1899 shows, because it represented an invasion of the private by the public sphere. The 'unwanted glances from outside' that entered with the light were an instance of the same social control that Michel Foucault has discussed in another context.[67] (In this context, incidentally, it made sense that the craze for country houses and cottages that began around 1900 made short shrift of heavy curtains, allowing outside light to stream into houses unimpared. For this light did not come from the street, but from nature, or even better, from one's own garden.)

To get back to artificial lighting, the unease about gas and electric light in the nineteenth century can now take its place in a larger setting. Like daylight, this sort of light had an outside source. Ostensibly burning in the middle of the room in the lamp, its real origin was in the gas-works or in the central electric supply station, that is in 'big industry', from which the bourgeois psyche tried to separate itself as it did from the public sphere. Just as the public sphere gained access to the home with daylight, so big industry forced its way in with the light of the gas flame and the electric bulb. The two combined in an uncanny way with the application of industrial lighting technology to public lighting. Gurlitt described what happened when it was no longer natural daylight that came in through the window, but harsh electric arc lighting: 'Many people who live in electri-

65. Orrinsmith, *The Drawing Room*, p. 64.

66. Karl Rosner, *Das deutsche Zimmer im 19. Jahrhundert* (Munich and Leipzig, 1899), p. 227 (also part of Hirth, *Das deutsche Zimmer*).

67. Michel Foucault, *Überwachen und Strafen* (Frankfurt, 1976), esp. the section on 'panoptism'.

cally lit streets have noticed its impact with alarm. They became most unpleasantly aware of the difference in colour between blue electric light and yellow gas- and lamp-light. These two forms of lighting are totally incompatible with each other. The harsh light of the new street lamps even penetrates into houses, forcing us to hang thick curtains in the windows.'[68]

68. Gurlitt, *Im Bürgerhaus*, p. 188.

The Stage

The whole manner in which stage sets have
generally been produced in the past will have
to change if electric light becomes established
in the theatre. The customary rough lines and
smudges will have to give way to more
polished representations executed with
greater finesse, and painted stage effects that
had a magical effect in the intimate light of
the gas flame will be condemned to disappear
in the presence of electric light.

(*Deutsche Bauzeitung*, 1882)

A wall and a chair are a great deal.

(Bertolt Brecht)

After a prologue in seventeenth-century Dutch painting, bourgeois realism conquered the stage in the second half of the
eighteenth century. The displays of splendour, the geometric
structures and the allegories and apotheoses of traditional baroque theatre struck the new sensibility as senselessly extravagant, chaotic and unnatural. The slogans under which the
eighteenth century cast off its baroque heritage were 'nature',
'imitation of nature', 'naturalness' and 'illusion'.

This new attitude is probably most apparent in the changes
made in the central perspective of the stage. Baroque stage sets
had been designed solely and exclusively with the ruler in mind;
his view of the stage was the only one from which the perspective 'worked'. 'The audience in the rest of the room was forced
to watch and participate from *above him* — as though they were
sitting over an esoteric high priest in front of the doors of the
inner sanctum.'[1] Eighteenth-century audiences no longer tolerated a view of the stage governed by absolutist eyes. What had
once been an expression of the accepted social order was now
seen to be merely a muddle, as described by Jean Baptiste
Pujoulx in his book, *Paris à la fin du 18e siècle*:

The perspective created by the set painter only makes sense from the

1. Rudolf zur Lippe, *Naturbeherrschung am Menschen*, Vol. 2 (Frankfurt, 1974), p. 25.

seat of one single spectator. Consequently, in an audience number-
ing 2,000 spectators, the 1,999 people who cannot sit in this seat find
that they are too close, too far away, too high, too low or too far to
the side. This turns stage sets designed along a central axis into a
system of confused and unrelated lines. They create a grotesque
structure, rather as if one were to turn the whole interior of a
drawing room upside down.[2]

Lighting for the baroque stage, which was above all lighting
for the central perspective, similarly came under fire in the
eighteenth century. Everything that happened on the stage was
to be a representation of nature — not only the acting, costumes
and scenery, but also the lighting that set everything else off.
Suddenly people realised that in its management of light the
stage had lagged far behind painting, which had been creating
impressive chiaroscuro effects for more than a hundred years.
Francesco Algarotti was one of the first theoreticians of the stage
to see the use of light in painting as a model for stage lighting.
'One does not know how to distribute it [i.e. light] evenly and
with economy,' he complained in 1750 of the lighting in contemporary theatres:

> The elements are poorly illuminated and always with insensitive
> shades, which do not make them stand out. Still, if they learnt the art
> of distributing the light, if it were to be concentrated *en masse* on
> some parts of the stage, excluding others, wouldn't it then transpose
> to the stage the power and vivacity of the clair-obsure that Rem-
> brandt succeeded in putting into his painting? It might even be
> possible to convey to the sceneries that delightful interplay of light
> and shade that you will find in Giorgione's and Titian's paintings.[3]

In 1760 the ballet master and choreographer Jean Georges
Noverre similarly condemned the symmetrical lighting of the
baroque stage, advocating instead an irregular, more natural
lighting:

> It is not the great number of lamps, used at haphazard or applied
> symmetrically that gives good light on the stage. The difficult thing is
> to be able to distribute the light unevenly so as to set off the parts that

2. Jean Baptiste Pujoulx, *Paris à la fin du 18ᵉ siècle* (Paris, 1801), p. 130.
3. Quoted from Gösta Bergman, *Lighting in the Theatre* (Stockholm, 1977), p. 178.

need strong light, to tone down where necessary and to put wholly in shadow where no light is needed. In the same way as the painter provides shades and degradations in his pictures for the sake of perspective, the person setting the light should consult him, so that the same shades and degradations can be seen in the lighting.[4]

Stage lighting as it developed in the baroque theatre remained essentially unchanged until well into the eighteenth century. Apart from its rigid, geometric arrangements, its lack of power made it incapable of living up to such dramaturgic demands. The seventeenth- and eighteenth-century stage is best described as a *frame of light*. It resembled a peep show in that it was not so much lit up from the sides as that its edges were marked or picked out by lights — in this, something like contemporary street lighting. The frame of light was created by lights in three positions: side lights, located in the proscenium arch and in the wings, footlights that lit up the actors from in front and below, and top lights, placed at the top of the proscenium arch and in the borders, and directed downwards by reflectors. Until the nineteenth century, however, top lighting was an exception,[5] as the available light sources were too weak to cast light effectively over the distance required. The same problem affected side lighting, but to a lesser extent, with the result that the centre of the stage suffered from a chronic lack of light. Side lighting simply did not reach the centre of the stage, which should have been the brightest spot. Instead, a channel of semi-darkness stretched from the apron to the back of the stage.

Under these conditions, the only effective lights were the footlights on the apron of the stage, where the distance separating them from the actors and the boards was smallest. All the same, footlights did not light up the whole stage either, but only a strip along the front of the stage. This is where most of the action took place — or, not to put too fine a point on it, this is where the actors jostled for space, competing for the light. For eighteenth-century aesthetics, which highly valued naturalness, this restriction was almost as bad as the other big disadvantage

4. Quoted from ibid., p. 180.
5. 'There is no evidence that top lighting was in constant and general use' (Carl-Friedrich Baumann, 'Entwicklung und Anwendung der Bühnenbeleuchtung seit der Mitte des 18. Jahrhunderts', dissertation, University of Cologne, 1956, p. 21).

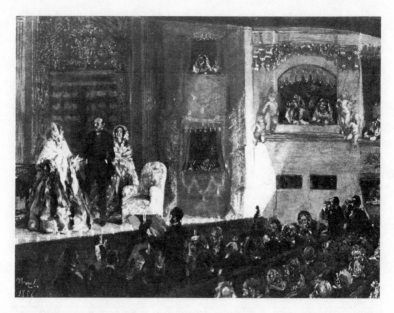

Footlights. 'Unfortunately, it is almost impossible to invent something better to replace this type of lighting, which lights the actors from below in a most unnatural, even unpleasant, way. . . . If we were to try directing the light down from above, the great distance would also prevent enough light from reaching the actors' (Louis Catel, 1802).
Adolph von Menzel, *Erinnerung an das Théâtre Gymnase in Paris* (Memory of the Théâtre Gymnase in Paris)
(Archiv für Kunst und Geschichte, Berlin)

of footlighting, namely that the light shone not from above like natural light, but from below. 'If we see the source of light at the actor's feet, do we not assume that it must be coming straight from Hell?' asks Pujoulx. He continues: 'After all, in nature, light always shines down from above, while in the theatre we are condemned to get it from Hell!'[6] Lit from below, actors' faces were distorted, to quote E.T.A. Hoffman, 'into grotesque masks' and 'our groups [of actors] resemble Chinese paintings, lacking composition and perspective — all because of this pre-

6. Pujoulx, *Paris à la fin du 18e siècle*, p. 128.

posterous lighting'.[7] This effect naturally made a mockery of the eighteenth-century art of physiognomical expression, as taught by Lavater. Footlighting was the only practicable form of lighting, but it was inherently distorting; this was the nub of the eighteenth-century public debate on the theatre. The actress Madame Riccoboni, for instance, tried to explain the actors' dilemma to her critic, Diderot, who had complained that the actors' habit of thronging on the forestage was unnatural. 'In an important scene', she wrote, 'the face contributes to the total expression. There are moments when a glance, or a slight inclination of the head, can be very meaningful. A smile can suggest that one is mocking the speaker, or trying to deceive the person one is speaking to. Looking straight ahead or lowering one's eyes can have a thousand different meanings. But if actors are more than three paces from the lights, nobody can see their faces.'[8]

As long as no stronger lights were available, footlights provided the only effective stage lighting. In 1802 the theatre architect Louis Catel summed up the situation:

> Unfortunately, it is almost impossible to invent something better to replace this type of lighting, which lights the actors from below in a most unnatural, even unpleasant, way. Attempts have been made to avoid this by using side lights attached to the walls of the proscenium, but because it is much too wide, not enough light reaches the centre of the stage. If we were to try directing the light down from above, the great distance would also prevent enough light from reaching the actors.[9]

Around 1800 it was technically impossible to replace footlighting by more natural light from above, but this did not stop people from theorising about it. Many ideas were suggested for top lighting, but they could not be put into practice until new techniques were developed in the late nineteenth century. Catel, for example, who had seemingly resigned himself to footlighting, also designed a theatrical project with side and top

---

7. Quoted from Baumann, 'Entwicklung und Anwendung der Bühnenbeleuchtung', p. 294.

8. Denis Diderot, *Oeuvres complètes*, Vol. 7 (Paris, 1875), p. 396.

9. Louis Catel, *Vorschläge zur Verbesserung der Schauspielhäuser* (Berlin, 1802), p. 18.

The spotlight is '. . . a concave metal mirror fixed in a position
where it gathers the light that would otherwise be lost and directs it
onto the stage or some other object. In this way all the light emitted
is made available for the object to be illuminated; none can escape'
(A.L. Lavoisier). (*Source*: *Académie des Sciences. Mémoires. Machines et
Inventions*, Paris, 1739; see illustration on p. 122.)

lighting. 'The sets are to be lit from the sides by six vertical,
standing rows of *réverbères*, and from the top by two rows of
horizontal, hanging *réverbères*. The purpose of this arrangement
is to concentrate the light on the centre of the set as much as
possible, where it has to be brightest, as in nature itself the
horizon and the air above it are most strongly lit up.'[10] Similarly,
in a project for a reformed theatre (1813), Schinkel proposed a
set consisting of a single, panorama-like backdrop instead of
wings and borders. His idea positively breathed open air *à la*
Caspar David Friedrich. Naturally, the light was to come from
above: 'By using . . . lighting from above, it is possible to make
the stage as a whole very light, without conferring too much
importance on the lower regions on which the actors walk.
Apart from this, light that falls from above has a much more
natural effect than light that rises from below.'[11]

10. Ibid., p. 17.
11. Quoted from Franz Benedikt Biermann, *Die Pläne für Reform des Theaterbaues bei Karl
Friedrich Schinkel und Gottfried Semper*, Schriften der Gesellschaft für Theatergeschichte, 38
(Berlin, 1928), p. 35.

Though it is true that really adequate top lighting only became possible with the introduction of gas and electric light, when Catel and Schinkel were designing their schemes, the Argand lamp, which had been invented in 1783, already made it possible to produce so much light that casting it over a greater distance seemed feasible for the first time.

To be effective, top lighting had to be brighter, but also more accurately directed. The flame naturally casts most of its light upwards and sideways; almost none of it goes downwards. To make light shine in this physically 'unnatural' direction required the artificial intervention of the reflector. Like Schinkel and Catel, Grobert, a French man of the theatre, thought that top lighting was the only natural form of lighting and that it was an objective to be pursued by all available means. He aspired to create 'such a blaze of light that the actors' every movement is visible', and proposed the following method: 'This effect can be achieved with the aid of large mirrors, and well-placed reflectors. This calls for detailed study and much experimentation.'[12]

In the second half of the eighteenth century the reflector became a crucial part of lighting technology, not only in the theatre but also in street lighting.

The novelty of the eighteenth-century reflector was its concave shape, which allowed it to collect, focus and concentrate — or in other terms, to 'discipline' — freely spreading light. The reflector lies at the heart of Lavoisier's two works on the theory of lighting, one on street lighting and one on lighting in the theatre. In the one on street lighting he defined the reflector as a 'concave metal mirror fixed in a position where it gathers the light that would otherwise be lost and directs it onto the stage or some other object. In this way all the light emitted is made available for the object to be illuminated; none can escape'.[13] In his proposal for improving theatre lighting he wrote: 'A reflector is nothing but a metal mirror which directs a mass of light that would otherwise disperse uselessly onto the object to be illuminated.'[14] The light of an oil lamp concentrated and directed by means of a concave reflector was the first clearly

12. Le Colonel Grobert, *De l'exécution dramatique* . . . (Paris, 1809), p. 224.

13. Lavoisier, *Oeuvres, Publiées par les soins de S. Exc. le ministre de l'instruction publique*, Vol. 3 (Paris, 1865), pp. 18–19.

14. Ibid., pp. 93–4.

recognisable kind of spotlight. With the introduction of electric light, it evolved into a crucial part of stage lighting. But even before the electric spotlight was fully developed, people could imagine an atmospheric distribution of light and shade, as in a painting. The defenders of the concave reflector in the eighteenth century stated explicitly that their aim was to use the beams of focused and directed light as a brush to create the most diverse effects. Lavoisier, for example, wrote: 'One can realistically evoke different moods and times of day: bright sunlight, the darkness of a thunderstorm, a sunrise or sunset, night time, full moon, etc. All this can be achieved very simply with the aid of parabolic or simple spherical reflectors fixed in the arch above the forestage.'[15] A contemporary of Lavoisier's, the architect Pierre Patte, had similar ideas. (Incidentally, he also put forward a suggestion for improving street lighting.) 'Our lighting would be improved so much by this method', he said about the reflector:

> Whether by shedding light on certain parts of the scene or by depriving others, sometimes you would reduce the brightness of the colours to produce a gentleness and harmony capable of charming the eyes of the spectator, sometimes one would cast on the stage those oppositions of light and shadow that are delightful in the paintings of the great masters and transport the piquant effects of clarity and obscurity onto the decorations.[16]

Patte was furthest ahead of his time in recognising the inherent potential of the reflector. He anticipated not only stage lighting from above and from the side, but also frontal lighting — something that only came with the development of electric spotlights.[17]

15. Ibid., p. 95.
16. Quoted from Bergman, *Lighting in the Theatre*, p. 402 (note 25).
17. 'All you would have to do would be to place three "lamp-posts" at intervals across the width of the auditorium close to the apron, three lamp-posts . . . at the end of the row of the second, third and fourth floors of boxes which from there could direct their light to good use and take in the tonality of the width and height of the proscenium in their rays. By these means, instead of being lit ridiculously from the bottom upwards, the objects on set would be lit from top to bottom as by the sun which would appear more natural. It is necessary to observe that given the position of these lamps behind the extremities of the row of boxes the spectators would not be inconvenienced by them — they would scarcely see them; they would merely rejoice in their brightness without seeing them. They would be turned on

By 1800 at the latest, natural light had conquered the stage. It was 'natural' in several senses: firstly, as actual light rather than an effect achieved by painted sets; secondly, as light from above rather than from below; and finally, in the very general sense in which this term was used by the bourgeois illusionist movement of the period for light that imitated moods created by natural light rather than illuminating geometric perspectives.

Suggestions made by theatre reformers in the late eighteenth and early nineteenth centuries went far beyond demands such as Algarotti's and Noverre's for a more painterly use of lighting, because they were expressed not merely in aesthetic terms but in precise technical ones. Patte's, Schinkel's, Catel's and Lavoisier's ideas were so detailed that all they needed to be put into practice was the invention of an appropriate light source. When lighting technology had advanced far enough in the nineteenth century with the aid of gas and electricity, these ideas were realised without further ado. The whole stage was lit up, including those parts that had previously been in semi-darkness. Footlighting was no longer an aesthetic problem. A report on the first use of gas for top lighting in a London theatre in 1817 mentioned 'a most agreeable and effectual light . . . upon the stage, where it tends to the correction of a very considerable evil, the unnatural and reversed lights produced by the footlights'.[18]

But around 1800 anticipating the new lighting theoretically was one thing; implementing it technically was another. As the new quantities of bright light poured over the stage, it almost collapsed under the onslaught. The new light mercilessly exposed all the old methods of creating illusions. What Paul Lindau said in the 1880s about the impression made by electric arc lighting was equally true of the first gas lighting: 'The disproportionately strong and intense light . . . washes out all the surrounding colours and because theatrical devices become crudely apparent in the bright light, it destroys all illusion. Instead of a tree one sees the painted canvas and instead of the

---

from the corridor and nothing would prevent their smoke from being funnnelled to just above the ceiling of the auditorium with the help of a simple little pipe made of tin plate.' Quoted from Bergman, *Lighting in the Theatre*, p. 403, note 26.

18. Quoted from Terence Rees, *Theatre Lighting in the Age of Gas* (London, 1978), p. 185.

A stage lit up by electric light
(Science Museum, London.)

sky, a sail cloth.'[19] In May 1883, when the Vienna Court Opera
experimentally used electric lighting, the reporter from the *Neue
Freie Presse* commented that the sets that had been 'produced to
a technically high standard' could continue to be used

> while simply painted or shabby sets could not pass the test of electric
> light. . . . All the flaws and defects are shown up in the bright
> light. . . . Today, for example, the effect of the cut-out backcloth
> from which twigs, festoons and ornaments freely hang down, held
> on by gauze, was greatly diminished because the electric light
> showed up its construction, its crude materiality and all the indis-
> pensable technical aids much too clearly.[20]

As the new light destroyed the illusion created by painted
sets, other tricks had to be found. They had to withstand the

19. Quoted from Baumann, 'Entwicklung und Anwendung der Bühnenbeleuchtung', p.
360.
20. *Neue Freie Presse*, 11 May 1883 (no. 6, 718).

effects of electric light and, what is more, to look especially realistic under it. Painted sets were replaced by naturalistic three-dimensional constructions that matched the 'naturalness' of electric spotlights. Colours, too, looked different in gas and electric light than in the light of candles and oil-lamps, and they had to be radically changed. In the Vienna Opera's experiment with electric light, the faces of singers made up in the traditional way — that is, for gaslight — looked too pale. It was concluded that 'under electric light more red has to be applied to achieve the same effect as under gas light'.[21] But colours did not only fade in brighter electric light. 'Some of the more mellow, richer colours, such as light green, violet and red, looked too garish. . . . Only muted, harmoniously co-ordinated colours appeared to better advantage than under gas light.'[22] In order to avoid disturbing effects, colours had to be attuned to the new light intensity — that is, made stronger, or darker and more muted as the case may be. The general trend was towards 'deeper, darker, more saturated' shades.[23] As early as 1827, it was noted that 'the late introduction of gas into our theatres has rendered a more powerful colouring than formerly used decidedly necessary'.[24]

Darker shades helped perfect the aesthetic illusion. For the first time, colours used on the stage were released from their old task of supporting the lighting, which had required brightness. As dark shades absorbed too much precious light, set painters had not been able to use them, even when aesthetic and realistic considerations demanded them. The colours of costumes are a good example. In the eighteenth century, costumes, like stage sets, were made of bright and shining colours. This offended Diderot's aesthetic sense, to pick one example. He wanted to see the bourgeois drama performed in bourgeois colours, that is, in unobtrusive dark shades which set them off clearly from the colourful, peacock-like display of the aristocracy. 'Splendour destroys everything', complains Diderot, 'the drama of splendour is not beautiful. Splendour . . . can dazzle the eye, but it

21. *Neues Wiener Tagblatt*, 11 May 1883 (no. 128).

22. Quoted from Baumann, 'Entwicklung und Anwendung der Bühnenbeleuchtung', p. 231.

23. Bergman, *Lighting in the Theatre*, p. 261.

24. Quoted from Rees, *Theatre Lighting*, p. 189.

cannot touch the heart. . . . The more serious a play, the more austere must be the costumes. . . . What we need is beautiful, simple clothes in unobtrusive colours.'[25] As Algarotti and Noverre took Dutch painting as a model for stage lighting, so Diderot suggested that actors learn from painting in the matter of costumes. He was probably thinking of portraits of Dutch burghers in dark suits. 'Actors! If you want to learn how to dress correctly, how to put aside false splendour and approach the sort of simplicity that alone can have the greatest impact, then visit our art galleries.'[26] As with his criticism of actors jostling for space at the front of the stage, here too Diderot rejected a practice made necessary by lighting technology as unnatural and unrealistic. Not until the nineteenth century, when the whole stage could be illuminated, did costumes and stage sets become as dark as the bourgeois taste in colours demanded. Not until then could actors leave the front of the stage and move around freely in the whole space available, without running the risk of disappearing in half-darkness.

In the nineteenth century the stage was gradually transformed by the new type of light. It responded to the new challenge and made use of the new potential on offer — real light banished the old illusion-creating art of set painting.

Set painting was attacked where it was weakest, in the presentation of light. In the seventeenth and eighteenth centuries, painted beams of light, painted shadows and painted dawns and sunsets had compensated for a lack of real light. They were accepted as natural because there was no other way to evoke these moods on the stage. According to Baumann: 'The atmosphere of a landscape and its characteristic outdoor light could only be achieved by painting.'[27] As soon as the Argand lamp provided the first efficient source of light on the stage, it proved to be a deadly rival for painted light. Pujoulx gives a nice description of the conflict between these two forms of light: 'If the scene painter has painted shadows and half-shadows on the sets and the person setting up the Argand lamps in the wings does not match them exactly, then the lighting man's system

25. Diderot, *Oeuvres complètes*, Vol. 7, pp. 375–6.
26. Ibid.
27. Baumann, 'Entwicklung und Anwendung der Bühnenbeleuchtung', p. 304.

clashes with the set painter's.'[28]

Losing the right to portray light was only the first defeat suffered by set painting. The other illusion-creating techniques it used also failed to survive under the new lighting regime. In general terms, the gradual replacement of painted sets by three-dimensional sets in the nineteenth century can be explained by the trend towards greater naturalism in the arts. But lighting led the way here, playing a real and perhaps even decisive part in this process. Actual light on the stage required ✓ an actual and not merely a painted space. Finally, with the aid of electric lights, Adolphe Appia was able to fulfil all the demands that had been made of theatre lighting more than 100 years before by Algarotti, Lavoisier and Patte. With Appia and his *living*, not painted, light, stage lighting became an independent creative medium:

> Appia's significance . . . lies in his perception that he was creating a real space that was activated by light. Performance space and light as new elements of the production are dependent on each other, as (active) light can only develop in a free space that is not 'destroyed' and cluttered up by painted sets. But space only becomes 'spatial' when light (and shade) became 'active' in it. The three-dimensionality of the actors, whose impact had been diminished by painted sets and who in turn had destroyed the effect of the painting, no longer contrasts with the free space and the terrain to which it gives shape; light and shade connect the actor with his 'action space'.[29]

The Darkening of the Auditorium

> I was immediately struck by an obvious drawback, namely that the relationship between stage lighting and auditorium lighting was totally wrong. The former was too weak and the latter too strong; the reverse would have been more correct and

28. Pujoulx, *Paris à la fin du 18ᵉ siècle*, p. 129.
29. Baumann, 'Entwicklung und Anwendung der Bühnenbeleuchtung', p. 422.

> better. This incongruity stems from the fact
> that the court pays for the auditorium light,
> while the theatre management pays for the
> stage lights.
> (August Klingemann, *Kunst und Natur*, 1823)

While new perceptions and lighting technology were trans-forming the stage, an equally significant metamorphosis was under way in the other half of the theatre. The auditorium that the eighteenth century inherited from the baroque theatre was more of a social, festive centre than a true auditorium. The audience gathered there not to concentrate on what was hap-pening on the stage but to participate in a double production. The performance on the stage was matched by one put on by the audience. To seventeenth-century perceptions, life itself was a universal theatre. Logically, therefore, the theatre consisted of two performance spaces of equal importance: the stage and the auditorium. As in baroque courtly festivals — processions, ballets, firework displays and illuminations — there was no clear dividing line between actors and audience. Everything was a game of entanglement and resolution. Roles were exchanged and confused and the narrow bounds of reality were burst, as in the contemporary hall of mirrors. Illumination made its contri-bution by lighting up the stage and the auditorium equally, the stage being marked out as a performance area only by a frame of light. The homogeneous nature of lighting in the baroque is perhaps most apparent in the fact that chandeliers decorated and illuminated both auditorium and stage. Seventeenth-century audiences were as little offended by chandeliers on the stage as by the lamp trimmers who went about their business on the open stage during the performance. Things that a little later were thought to destroy the illusion and were therefore re-garded as unacceptable were simply part of the performance in the baroque theatre. 'In France, the *moucheurs* were popular people whose presence was welcomed. If they carried out their work carefully and elegantly, the audience would greet them with applause or words of praise.'[30]

Around the middle of the eighteenth century, audiences began to feel that this communication between stage and audi-

30. Ibid. p. 15.

Stage and auditorium during the *ancien régime*. G.P. Panini, *Die Aufführung der Oper Contesa dei Numi in Rom* (Performance of the Opera Contesa dei Numi in Rome), 1729
(Archiv für Kunst und Geschichte, Berlin)

torium was aesthetically and morally displeasing. A clear boundary was drawn between them. In the baroque theatre, steps had connected the stage with the auditorium, and actors had often made their entries on them. Now they disappeared, and the seats for the audience that had been allowed on the stage itself were also cleared away. Chandeliers, too, lost their place on the stage, which was now seen as an autonomous space for creating aesthetic illusions that was strictly separated from the audience. In the Comédie Française, seats and chandeliers were banished from the stage in 1757. After this date they were only allowed on the stage as props.

The loss of chandeliers did not mean that the stage was less brightly lit. On the contrary, throughout the eighteenth century the trend was clearly towards a brighter stage and a darker auditorium. At the beginning of the eighteenth century, the auditorium of the Comédie Française was lit by twelve chandeliers with 136 candles. Fifty years later, just before chandeliers disappeared from the stage, there were only four chandeliers with forty-eight candles, amounting to one-third of the previous illuminating power. At the same time, stage lighting multiplied from forty-eight candles in the wings in 1719 to 116 in 1757. In addition, of course, there were the reflector lamps that did not exist at the beginning of the eighteenth century; by the 1750s they were the most important light source.[31]

It had long been known that the more brightly a picture is lit and the darker the position from which it is observed, the more distinct it appears. Renaissance theoreticians of the theatre had already used this insight. Di Somi, for instance, recommended placing the audience in shadow 'the reason being that the sight proceeds more directly and without any distraction toward his object, or, according to the peripatetic theory, the object impinges itself more directly upon the eye'.[32] And Ingegneri laid down the following rule of thumb: 'The darker the auditorium, the more luminous seems the stage.'[33]

This perception, however, had no practical effect on the Renaissance and the baroque theatre, as the social role of the theatre demanded a brightly lit auditorium. The fact that the auditorium gradually got darker as the stage grew brighter throughout the eighteenth century signalled that a change was taking place in the social, aesthetic and moral role of the theatre. The audience that assembled in the auditorium now directed all its attention to the events on the stage. In essence, it was no longer 'an audience', but a large number of individuals, each of whom followed the drama for him or herself. The new ideal was to achieve direct communication between the spectator and what was being presented, to the exclusion of all distracting, external factors. The idea of darkening the auditorium was to enhance this feeling of community between the viewer and the drama by shutting out the social phenomenon of the audience

31. All these details in Bergman, *Lighting in the Theatre*, pp. 170–1.
32. Quoted from ibid., p. 64.
33. Quoted from ibid., p. 66.

for the duration of the play. According to Brecht, this sums up the development of the theatre over the last 200 years. But on closer inspection, it turns out that the story is not quite as simple and straightforward as this dictum suggests. The process of darkening the auditorium was slow; it proceeded by fits and starts. Above all, it was never completed. Despite everything, the theatre as an institution basks in its own light, as a look at the most remarkable outgrowth of the Italian theatre, the opera, shows.

Opera demonstrates that a darkened auditorium does not necessarily go hand in hand with the aesthetics of realism and illusion. In Italian opera, a darkened auditorium had been the norm since the seventeenth century, long before it was adopted in other European theatres. Nevertheless, Italian audiences were anything but disciplined consumers of art. They watched the performance as distractedly as did opera audiences in Paris, London and Vienna, for like them, Italian audiences put themselves on show. They could do this in a darkened auditorium because in the Italian opera the auditorium was not really what it seemed, but a transitional space. The real auditorium was divided up into numerous boxes — an Italian, originally Venetian, invention:

> The auditorium was a collective of boxes separated by solid side walls, rooms with three walls, and if they wished, a fourth with shutters that could be closed towards the auditorium. . . . The tiers of boxes were a kind of semi-detached house. Each family with their company had a 'chambre séparée', furnished with their own taste as a *boudoir* with wallpaper, paintings, mirrors, small tables, chairs, couches, possibly also gambling tables. People made conversation, supped, played cards and made frequent calls on each other.[34]

Italian audiences were just as inattentive towards what was happening on the stage as were other European audiences, the only difference being that their cult of society took place in a large number of small rooms. In Italy, the space in front of the stage was not an auditorium that was darkened for aesthetic reasons, but an undefined middle ground stretching between the brightly lit stage and the similarly illuminated boxes. The

---

34. Ibid., p. 89.

matter is complicated, however, by the fact that this space was also an auditorium after all, in the sense that this is where the lower classes consorted. But they did not belong to 'society', and followed their own rules of behaviour. Here, darkness did not have the effect of promoting concentration and quietness. On the contrary, 'the semi-darkness of the auditorium of course did nothing to increase the order of the pit, filled largely as it was with a popular audience of gondoliers and other categories. . . . Foreign visitors were amazed at the life in the pit, the liberties taken, the loud conversations and the row, the selling of fruit and refreshments.'[35]

In French, English and central European theatres it is true that as auditoriums gradually grew darker, the concentration of audiences increased. The darkness of the auditorium was a reliable indicator of the degree of illusionism. But the practice of darkening the auditorium spread only slowly and against great resistance. Watelet-Levêque commented in 1793 that the audience 'wanted to see the stage, wanted to see the actors; but above all, they wanted to see each other and, if we may say so, to take in every detail.'[36] And in 1809 Grobert wrote: 'I do not think that a single artist would object if the chandeliers that illuminate French auditoriums at the expense of the stage were to be removed. But everyone argues against this useful reform by saying that the women want to be seen, and that the public wants to see them.'[37]

Theatre reformers also advocated a new lighting regime for the auditorium. Three methods were proposed. The first was to shield the auditorium lights behind a screen — a technique that had already been used in the baroque theatre to create special lighting effects. Pujoulx' suggestion follows these lines: 'One could solve the dilemma posed by auditorium lights and the requirements of the stage by covering up the chandelier during the performance, so that it only gives off a weak glow. Thus the

35. Ibid., p. 90.

36. Quoted from Baumann, 'Entwicklung und Anwendung der Bühnenbeleuchtung', p. 61; also in Johann Adam Breysig, *Skizzen, Gedanken, Entwürfe, Umrisse, Versuche, Studien, die bildenden Künste betreffend* (Magdeburg, 1800), p. 71. (This is largely a paraphrase of C.-H. Watelet and P.C. Levesques, *Dictionnaire des Arts de Peinture, Scripture et Gravure*, Paris, 1792.)

37. Grobert, *De l'exécution dramatique*, p. 265.

stage would get the light it needs. During the interval, the chandelier could be uncovered again.'[38] Grobert suggested that the lights scattered around the auditorium should be screened by 'metal hoods, that would partially or completely cover the light. Lifting them would make the light brighter; lowering them would make it darker.'[39] The second method of moderating auditorium lights, one that was in general use from the end of the eighteenth century on, was to have only one, central chandelier. At the beginning of the performance it was hoisted up, sometimes disappearing completely into a space in the ceiling, and during intervals it was lowered again. The third method, finally, was to use reflector lamps attached to the ceiling. Eighteenth-century theatre reformers such as Patte, Lavoisier and Cochin, who also favoured top lighting for the stage, argued for the use of these *plafond lumineux*. Like top lighting, the *plafond lumineux* could not be implemented until new lighting techniques became available in the nineteenth century.

None of these methods aimed to make the auditorium completely dark. All they wanted to achieve was a dimmer light, a 'mild and soft brightness', as Patte puts it.[40] The central chandelier seems to have provided exactly the compromise that was needed. On the one hand, it met the need for illusion by disappearing from view during the performance and reducing the amount of light. On the other, it embodied the festive character of the theatre. The social desire to see and be seen has survived in the theatre, despite illusionism, realism and naturalism. Even when gas and electric light brought a total blackout within easy reach, European auditoriums were not plunged into darkness, but only into a dusky light. Werner Siemens, who provided electric lighting systems for many theatres, advised that when the curtain went up, 'the auditorium should be lit mildly and, like the stage, only by a reddish light. To achieve this, simply place one or more rings of lights on the galleries, where they stay on all the time'.[41]

Auditorium lighting is a reliable guide to the social character

38. Pujoulx, *Paris à la fin du 18ᵉ siècle*, p. 129.
39. Grobert, *De l'exécution dramatique*, p. 267.
40. Quoted from Baumann, 'Entwicklung und Anwendung der Bühnenbeleuchtung', p. 104.
41. Quoted from ibid., p. 271.

The central chandelier, Académie royale de musique, Paris
(*Source*: Pugin and Heath, *Paris and Its Environs*.)

of any particular theatre. Richard Wagner's performances at
Bayreuth took place before an almost totally darkened auditorium. This was a radical attempt to abolish the theatre as a social
place and to transform it into a mystical one. But the social
instincts of the audience resisted this bid to suppress an ancient
function of the theatre, perhaps less in Germany, where there
was a tradition of aesthetic experiences replacing social ones,
than in western European capitals such as London. 'When at last
in the 1890s house lights were extinguished at Covent Garden
while the curtain was up there was still resistance from the old
habitués who objected sitting through *Der Ring des Nibelungen* in a
darkened auditorium which demanded and focused their attention to the stage.'[42] The 'mystical abyss' that Wagner wanted to
open up between the stage and the auditorium remained a mere
episode in the history of the theatre. In the twentieth century all
progressive theories of the theatre have aimed to 'fill in the
orchestra' (to quote Walter Benjamin on Brecht's epic theatre).

42. Rees, *Theatre Lighting*, p. 188.

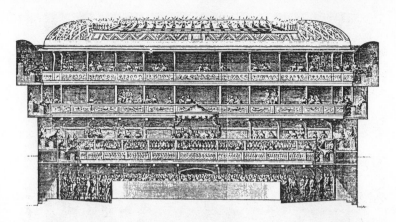

The plafond lumineux. (1) Eighteenth-century project for a ceiling illumination using candles.
(2) Electrical *plafond lumineux*, around 1883.
(*Source*: Cochin, *Lettres sur l'Opéra*, Paris, 1781; *La Lumière électrique*, 1883)

The nineteenth-century auditorium. The Grand Theatre in
Moscow, festively illuminated, 1856. Coloured lithograph.
(Archiv für Kunst und Geschichte, Berlin.)

They propose to revive the open, communicative relationship
between the stage and the audience that existed in the seventeenth and eighteenth centuries before the victory of illusionism. The darkened auditoriums of most twentieth-century
theatres are not the result of any passionate aesthetic vision
such as Wagner's — at most, they are the final, mechanical
reflex of such a vision. Or, more simply, the darkened auditorium of the municipal theatre reflects the waning of its social role.
Indeed, this darkness may even be a carry-over from an aesthetic institution quite separate from the theatre. It has been suggested that 'the obligatory darkening of cinema auditoriums
helped to establish this practice as the norm'.[43] The stubborness
with which light has retained a place in theatre auditoriums
speaks for this view. This would mean that the darkness that
reigns today is an import, something quite alien to the theatre
itself. In the evolution of darkened cinemas, illusionism took a
very different line of development, one quite independent of the
theatre.

43. Baumann, 'Entwicklung und Anwendung der Bühnenbeleuchtung', p. 279.

Panorama, Diorama and Magic Lantern

> Daguerre nous a fait entrer dans l'intérieur
> des tableaux, dont, avant lui, on ne voyait
> que la surface.
>
> (Jules Janin, 1839)

Eighteenth and nineteenth-century theatres tried to imitate the use of light in painting, and this led to a struggle between stage lighting and set painting. In the end, set painting was vanquished and lighting finally took over the stage as a medium of spatial expression. The auditorium was only darkened with reluctance, for the old communicative, social relationship between the stage and the audience proved resistant to change. There can be no doubt that the new perceptions of light in the eighteenth century and the new lighting technology of the nineteenth century revolutionised the theatre. But the resistance that had to be overcome suggests that the greatest triumphs of the new light as a medium of illusion did not take place in the theatre.

In fact, around 1800 several completely new media developed, in which light was the most important element in the creation of illusion. In them, new eighteenth- and nineteenth-century perceptions of light created their own, so to speak, institutional forms instead of, as in the case of theatre lighting, merely infiltrating an existing institution and changing it in the teeth of fierce opposition. The new media of the nineteenth century — the panorama, the diorama, the magic lantern, 'dissolving views' and, finally, film — were pure aesthetic, technical creations born of the spirit of light. The main difference between them and the theatre was that they created a pictorial instead of a spatial illusion. They were an extension of painting rather than the stage. Light could achieve a more perfect effect in these new media than on the stage because it did not have to compete with a painting, but instead heightened its effect. The use of light to enliven a two-dimensional painted illusion was not susceptible to the sorts of breaks in illusion that were inherent in the theatre with its mixture of pictorial and spatial elements. The picture world of the new media offered endless opportunities for creating illusions, belonging as it did to a different existential sphere

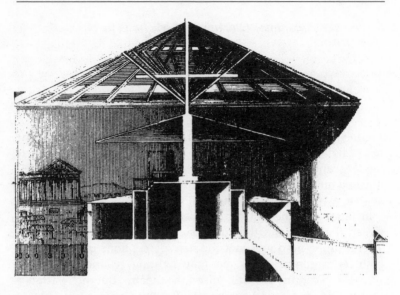

Cross-section through a panorama (1816).
(*Source*: S. Oettermann, *Panorama*.)

from the reality in which the audience was sitting. The mystical abyss that even Wagner could not fully conjure up opened of its own accord between every fairground panorama and its audience.

The first of the new light-based media was the panorama, which developed around 1800.[44] It used light in a very restrained manner. Breaking open the frame and releasing the image from its limitations was still the job of the painting itself — cast in cylindrical form with no side edges, it was complete in itself, the beginning always connected with the end. While painting could solve this problem, other means had to be found to dissolve the top and bottom edges of the picture. Here the panorama did pioneering work for later light-based media by placing spectators in half darkness in a position from which the picture appeared to be continuous. 'Viewers looked at the pic-

44. Here we can do no more than refer to Stephan Oettermann's study, *Das Panorama: Die Geschichte eines Massenmediums* (Frankfurt, 1980) — the most comprehensive, knowledgeable and profound of the books on the subject.

ture from a platform in the middle of the room that was about half as high as the picture. Light came in through an opening in the ceiling, hidden from the spectator by a roof above the platform. This roof also obscured the top edge of the canvas. Similarly, the bottom edge was invisible, hidden by a cloth stretched between the platform and the canvas. Wherever it looked, the audience, in the shadow of the roof above its head, could see nothing but brightly illuminated canvas.'[45] The space between the audience and the picture was taken up by an empty passageway, half in darkness and lined top and bottom with cloth, presumably black. Its function was to bridge, or rather, to transform this space. The effect of this space was to transfer the picture into a sphere that was not part of the observer's world; at the same time, the viewer was mysteriously drawn close to the picture, indeed, psychologically drawn into it. A report of 1800 investigating the effect of panoramas on the people watching them states: 'As there is not a single object that could serve as a comparison, the viewer experiences the most perfect illusion. It is not a picture that he sees, but nature itself unfolding before his eyes.'[46] All contemporary descriptions of the panorama mention its power of suggestion over the viewer. It seemed to take possession of his eyes. He became helpless and lost his bearings because the normal points of reference were missing. Critics of the panorama describe this effect. J.A. Eberhard experienced 'dizziness and nausea' caused by the

> impossibility of withdrawing from the delusion. I feel as though I am chained to it with iron bands. The inconsistency between illusion and reality seizes me; I want to tear myself free by destroying the treacherous illusion, but I feel that I am ensnared in the web of an inconsistent dream world. Neither the assurance of my feelings at the distance of the viewing platform, nor bright daylight, nor a comparison with the bodies around me can awaken me from the anxious dream which I am compelled to continue dreaming against my will. Someone who has been deluded can use these means to put an end to the illusion as soon as it begins to be unpleasant, but they are not available to the audience of a panorama.[47]

45. Heinz Buddemeier, *Panorama, Diorama, Photographie. Entstehung und Wirkung neuer Medien im 19. Jahrhundert* (Munich, 1970), p. 17.
46. Quoted from ibid., p. 166.
47. Quoted from ibid., p. 175.

The diorama, first presented to the public in 1822 by Daguerre and Bolton, was an instant success. It used light in a much more sophisticated way than the panorama, and the illusion it created was based on a completely different principle. While the panorama consisted of a cylindrical picture, the diorama offered a peep-show view. The illusion was created not by the continuous nature of the image, but by a changing spectacle produced by lighting changes. 'The most striking effect is the change of light', reported *The Times* about Daguerre's diorama 'Valley of Sarnen'.

> From a calm, soft, delicious, serene day in summer, the horizon gradually changes, becoming more and more overcast, until a darkness, not the effect of night, but evidently of approaching storm — a murky, tempestuous blackness — discolours every object, making us listen almost for the thunder which is to growl in the distance, or fancy we feel the large drops, the avant-couriers of the shower. This change of light upon the lake (which occupies a considerable portion of the picture) is very beautifully contrived. The warm reflection of the sunny sky recedes by degrees, and the advancing dark shadow runs across the water. . . .[48]

The diorama with its realistic effects was described as follows by Buddemeier:

> Every picture in a diorama — there are always two on display — was 22 metres high and 14 metres wide. Colour was applied to a transparent screen using a technique developed by Daguerre, which gave an opaque or translucent finish according to the effect desired. Light was provided by both top lighting in front of the picture and by windows at the back of the building, where several screens of various colours could be adjusted to regulate the amount of light coming in. Viewers sat in a room rather like a theatre, with stepped rows of seating, that was almost completely dark. The front row was 13 metres from the picture on display; this distance was spanned by a tunnel draped in black, which gave the same effect as an unframed peep show.[49]

Although the panorama and the diorama functioned diffe-

48. Quoted from Helmut and Alison Gernsheim, *L.J.M. Daguerre: The History of the Diorama and the Daguerrotype* (London, 1965), p. 15.
49. Buddemeier, *Panorama, Diorama, Photographie.*, pp. 25-6.

Diorama (1848)
(*Source*: Oettermann, *Panorama*.)

rently, they had a common element in the space, lined with black cloth, that lay between the audience and the picture. Buddemeier called it a tunnel, a *visual tunnel*. In the panorama, this space had been as circular as the picture itself, and had only been half darkened. But in the diorama, it became a real tunnel and was pitch black. The visual tunnel was the optical device √ which created the illusion of infinity. It was a further development, on a much larger scale, of course, of the peep show and the kaleidoscope. Common to all these optical devices and the diorama was that they cancelled the visual distance and made the viewer feel that he was right inside the picture. Auerbach wrote that this made it possible

> apparently to sweep away the boundaries, for the viewer, of a picture that is, in fact, bounded. This effect is achieved by removing the frame from the picture and, after reducing it to a greater or lesser degree, placing it in front of the picture. The frame thus becomes an aperture for looking through, and the picture lying behind it appears to the spectator to be unlimited, while its 'visibility' is effectively heightened.[50]

50. Alfred Auerbach, *Panorama und Diorama. Ein Abriß über Geschichte und Wesen*

Similar techniques, incidentally, were used in the theatrical projects designed by Catel and Schinkel. Schinkel himself also painted panoramas and dioramas.[51] A backcloth, designed by Catel, had panorama-like dimensions: it was to be 18 metres (60 feet) high and 55 metres (180 feet) wide, and framed in such a way 'that even those members of the audience sitting closest to the proscenium cannot see its top or side edges'.[52] A project by Schinkel even more clearly resembled a diorama. Van Alst writes that 'Schinkel's sets and the diorama follow the same principles of construction: (1) the fixed aperture, (2) fixed side walls, the "visual tunnel", (3) the illusionist "painting", the actual set.'[53] These ideas, however, were not put into practice on the stage of about 1800. The example of Daguerre shows that the old medium of the theatre was not the most suitable place to develop these new illusion-creating techniques.

Daguerre started his career as a painter of stage scenery. He was famous for his sets and especially his lighting effects long before he was immortalised by the daguerrotype. In contemporary reviews, it was often the set painter who was singled out for special praise, not the composer or librettist.[54] Daguerre laid the foundations for the new medium in the old. 'Daguerre's stage sets for *Eloide* clearly used techniques that were perfected at a later date in the diorama. We can recognise all the characteristic features of the diorama: the visual tunnel, in this case a real stage, that has continuous walls and is usable. Because of the dark foreground, the illuminated backdrop has a much stronger illusionist effect than it would have on an ordinary stage.'[55]

volkstümlicher Wirklichkeitskunst (Grimmen, 1942), quoted from Marianne Mildenberger, *Film und Projektion auf der Bühne* (Emsdetten, Westphalia, 1961), p. 22.

51. Baumann, 'Entwicklung und Anwendung der Bühnenbeleuchtung', p. 318. 'It has been shown that some of Schinkel's well-known paintings and theatre sets were based on his panoramas; and conversely, that dioramas were modelled on his paintings' (Kurt Karl Eberlein, 'Diorama, Panorama und Romantik', *Das Nationaltheater*, vol. 1, no. 4 (1928/9), p. 37). 'Schinkel's experience as a panorama painter prepared him for his new career as a theatre artist. The mastery of his theatre sets . . . is inconceivable without this peculiar type of visual art' (ibid., p. 38).

52. Catel, *Vorschläge zur Verbesserung der Schauspielhäuser*, pp. 5–6.

53. Theo van Alst, 'Gestaltungsprinzipien des szenischen Naturalismus', dissertation, University of Cologne, 1954, quoted from Mildenberger, *Film und Projektion auf der Bühne*, p. 23.

54. Gernsheim, *L.J.M. Daguerre* (New York: Dover edn), p. 12.

55. Van Alst, 'Gestaltungsprinzipien des szenischen Naturalismus', quoted from Baumann, 'Entwicklung und Anwendung der Bühnenbeleuchtung', p. 312.

Daguerre eventually stopped working for the stage, as it was too small to contain the powerful illusions he created with light. Actors, language and plot were incompatible with this new illusionism. After his first successes with the two-dimensional diorama, Daguerre developed a new variety with a three-dimensional foreground. This, however, did not go down well — proof that actual space always destroys a perfect illusion of space. The magical transformation of a painting into an illusion of reality took place through the visual tunnel. (Wagner's 'mystical abyss' had a similar purpose.)[56]

The magic lantern and 'dissolving views' can be described as a connecting link between the diorama and film. They followed the same rules, as did film itself. The only difference was that the painted picture was replaced by a projected and animated picture. The crucial thing remained that the viewer sat in the dark and watched an illuminated scene. 'You are in a dark room. Suddenly, a big window opens. What do you see? A picture? No, nature itself.'[57] This description of one of Daguerre's dioramas, published in 1826 by the Saint-Simonian journal, *Globe*, captures the impression made by each of the subsequent light-based media in the nineteenth and twentieth centuries. Similarly, Jules Janin's comment that Daguerre had opened up the way into the interior of the picture is matched, 100 years later, by Bela Balász' description of the film image: 'The camera takes my eye with it. Right into the middle of the image. I see

---

56. Wagner described the 'empty space between the proscenium and the audience' that resulted from his 'demand that the orchestra be invisible' as a mystical abyss. He felt that this was an appropriate name 'because it has to separate reality from ideality'. The two proscenium arches, one in front of the orchestra and one behind it, create a kind of visual tunnel at the Festspielhaus in Bayreuth. This makes possible 'the wonderful illusion that the actual scene is moving further away. . . . It is created by the fact that the spectators think that what is happening on the stage is far away, while they perceive it with all the clarity of actual proximity; this gives rise to a further illusion, namely that the people appearing on stage are of superhuman stature. The success of this arrangement alone should be enough to give some idea of the incomparable effect of the relationship thus created between spectator and stage. As soon as the spectators are sitting in their seats, they find themselves in a virtual 'theatron', that is, a space designed solely for looking at what can be seen from its seats. Between the spectators and the scene to be observed nothing is clearly visible; there is only a 'space', kept indeterminate by architectural mediation, between the two prosceniums, presenting the distanced image in all the inaccessability of a dream vision' (R. Wagner, 'Bayreuth, das Bühnenfestspielhaus', in *Sämtliche Schriften und Dichtungen*, Volksausgabe, Leipzig, n.d., Vol. 9, pp. 337–8).

57. *Globe*, 1826, quoted from Buddemeier, *Panorama, Diorama, Photographie*, p. 182.

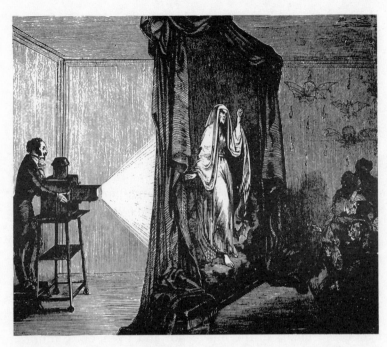

Magic lantern (1885). 'The camera takes my eye with it. Right into the middle
of the image. I see things from the perspective of the space created by the
film. I am surrounded by the figures of the film and involved in its action
that I see from all sides' (Bela Balász).
(Archiv für Kunst und Geschichte, Berlin.)

things from the perspective of the space created by the film. I am
surrounded by the figures of the film and involved in its action
that I see from all sides.'[58]

Common to all these media, from the diorama to the cinema-
scope screen, is a darkened auditorium and a brightly illuminated image. These have remained constant despite all the
technical changes of the last 150 years. In light-based media,
light does not simply illuminate existing scenes; it creates them.
The world of the diorama and the cinema is an illusory dream
world that light opens up to the viewer. He can lose himself in it

58. Bela Balász, *Der Geist des Films* (reprinted Munich, 1983), pp. 9–10.

in the same way that he can submerge himself in contemplating the flame of a camp-fire or a candle. In this respect, the film is closer to the fire than to the theatre. An open-air performance in bright daylight is quite feasible, while a camp-fire in the light of day is as senseless, even invisible, as a film projected in day-light. The power of artificial light to create its own reality only reveals itself in darkness. In the dark, light is life. The spectator sitting in the dark and looking at an illuminated image gives it his whole attention — one could almost say, his life. The illuminated scene in darkness is like an anchor at sea. This is the root of the power of suggestion exercised by the light-based media since Daguerre's time. The spectator in the dark is alone with himself and the illuminated image, because social connec-tions cease to exist in the dark. Darkness heightens individual perceptions, magnifying them many times. The darkened audi-torium gives the illuminated image an intensity that it would not otherwise possess. Every lighted image is experienced as the light at the end of the tunnel — the visual tunnel, in this case — and as a liberation from the dark.

Select Bibliography

d'Allemagne, H.-R., *Histoire du luminaire*, Paris, 1891

Bachelard, G., *La Flamme d'une chandelle*, Paris, 1961

Bader, L., 'Gas Illumination in New York City, 1823–1863', dissertation, New York University, 1970

Bell, L., *The Art of Illumination*, New York, 1902

Bergman, G., *Lighting in the Theatre*, Stockholm, 1977

Besnard, B., *L'Industrie du gaz à Paris depuis ses origines*, Paris, 1942

Bryan, G.S., *Edison: The Man and His Work*, London and New York, 1926

Buddemeier, H., *Panorama, Diorama, Photographie. Entstehung and Wirkung neuer Medien im 19. Jahrhundert*, Munich, 1970

Cardon, E., *L'Art au foyer domestique*, Paris, 1884

Chandler, D., *Outline of History of Lighting by Gas*, London, 1936

Chandler, D., and Lacey, A.D., *The Rise of the Gas Industry in Britain*, London, 1949

Citron, P., *La Poésie de Paris dans la littérature française de Rosseau à Baudelaire*, Vol. 1, Paris, 1961

Clegg, S., Jr, *A Practical Treatise on the Manufacture and Distribution of Coal-Gas*, 1st edn, London, 1841

Davis, D., *A History of Shopping*, London and Toronto, 1966

Davy, Humphry, *Elements of Chemical Philosophy*, London, 1812, Vol. 1

Defrance, E., *Histoire de l'éclairage des rues de Paris*, Paris, 1904

Facey, J.W., *Practical House Decoration*, London, 1886

Foster, G.G., *New York by Gas-Light*, New York, 1850

Fürst, A., *Das elektrische Licht*, Munich, 1926

Galine, L., *Traité général d'éclairage*, Paris, 1894

Gernsheim, A., and Gernsheim, H., *L.J.M. Daguerre: The History of the Diorama and the Daguerrotype*, London, 1965

Gurlitt, C., *Im Bürgerhaus*, Dresden, 1888

Harris, J.R., 'The Rise of Coal Technology', *Scientific American*, August 1974

Hassenstein, C.H., *Das elektrische Licht*, Weimar, 1859

Hausenstein, W., *Licht unter dem Horizont. Tagebücher von 1942 bis 1946*, Munich, 1967

Havard, H., *La Décoration*, Paris, n.d.

Herlaut (Commandant), 'L'Eclairage des rues à Paris a la fin du 17ᵉ au 18ᵉ siècles', *Société de l'Histoire de Paris et de l'Ille-de-France. Mémoires*, Vol. 43

Hirth, G., *Das deutsche Zimmer der Gotik und Renaissance, des Barock-,*

Rokoko- und Zopfstils, Munich and Leipzig, 1899

Hunt, C., *A History of the Introduction of Gas Lighting*, London, 1907

Knaggs, N.S., *Adventures in Man's First Plastic*, New York, 1947

Lavoisier, A.L., *Oeuvres*, Vol. 3, Paris, 1865

Lotz, A., *Das Feuerwerk*, Leipzig, n.d. [1940]

Maitland, W., *The History and Survey of London*, Vol. 1, London, 1760

Matthews, W., *An Historical Sketch of the Origin, Progress and Present State of Gas-Lighting*, London, 1827

Mildenberger, M., *Film und Projektion auf der Bühne*, Emsdettten, Westphalia, 1961

Nahrstedt, W., *Die Entstehung der Freizeit, dargestellt am Beispiel Hamburgs*, Göttingen, 1972

Nef, J.U., *Rise of the British Coal Industry*, 2 vols., London, 1932

Orrinsmith, Mrs, *The Drawing Room, Its Decoration and Furniture*, in the series 'Art at Home', London, 1878

Parville, H., de, *L'Electricité et ses applications*, 2nd edn, Paris, 1883

Peckston, T.S., *The Theory and Practice of Gas-Lighting*, London, 1819

Peclet, E., *Die Kunst der Gebäude- Zimmer- und Straßenbeleuchtung durch Oel, Talg, Wachs und Gas*, Weimar, 1853

Pugin, A., and Heath, C., *Paris and its Environs*, London, 1831

Pujoulx, J.P., *Paris à la fin du 18ᵉ siècle*, Paris, 1801

Rees, T., *Theatre Lighting in the Age of Gas*, London, 1978

Rodenberg, J., *Paris bei Sonnenschein und Lampenlicht*, Leipzig, 1867

Rumford, Count B., *The Complete Works*, Vol. 4, Boston, n.d.

Rutter, J.O.N., *Gas-Lighting: Its Progress and Its Prospects*, London, 1849

Salusbury-Jones, G.T., *Street Life in Medieval England*, Brighton, 1975 (1st edn 1939)

Schilling, N.H., *Handbuch für Steinkohlengas-Beleuchtung*, 2nd edn, Munich, 1866

Schöne, W., *Über das Licht in der Malerei*, 4th edn, Berlin, 1977

Schroeder, M., *The Argand Burner: Its Origin and Development in France and England 1780–1859*, Odense, 1969

Scott, W.S., *Green Retreats: The Story of Vauxhall Gardens 1661–1859*, London, 1955

Stevenson, Robert Louis, 'A Plea for Gas Lamps', in *The Travels and Essays*, Vol. 13, New York, 1917

Sydney, W.C., *England and the English in the 18th Century*, London, 1892

Trébuchet, A., *Recherches sur l'éclairage public de Paris*, Paris, 1843

Whipple, F.H., *Municipal Lighting*, Detroit, 1888

Wroth, W., *The London Pleasure Gardens of the 18th Century*, London, 1896

Index of Persons